A Homegrown Table

To my beautiful and supportive family for their ongoing support and to wonderful Dan for simply believing in me.

A Homegrown Table

FOOD TO EAT WITH FAMILY AND FRIENDS

NEW HOLLAND

EMMA DEAN

Contents

Introduction

My passion for all things planting, growing and harvesting started at a very young age. For as long as I can remember I have been rummaging around in the garden beds, learning to appreciate nature's bounty and understand the seasons. Greenfingers? Or maybe just muddy fingers!

One of my earliest memories was helping my dad plant pumpkin seeds in the dry, hot central Victorian soil. Using my small hand as a template, I spaced the precious seeds 10 hands apart. I covered the seeds with crumbly soil and watered them in. After what seemed an eternity, small green shoots started to appear out of the soil. It should have been fragile, but in fact this incredibly robust seedling burst into my life! At the end of summer, our family would have an abundance of large pumpkins, which we'd store in a cool, dark place, to last us through winter. Needless to say, I loved pumpkins when I was little, mainly because I grew them.

Both my parents were teachers and taught my sisters and me to cook seasonally, how to knead bread and how to grow food. We had a small farm in Bendigo where we bred cows and horses and had goats, sheep and chickens. We knew what a good lamb chop and a homegrown tomato tasted like.

My parents loved to hold big parties in the hayshed, with a delicious piece of meat roasting on a spit over a fire. When I moved out of the family home with my sisters, we also loved entertaining, having people around, and throwing parties. As students we also learnt that seasonal food was cheaper. We would often buy a tray of avocados and make guacomole for a Mexican fiesta; mangoes for mango daiquiris, roasted chestnuts in winter—even our party menus back then were influenced by the seasons!

I am heavily influenced by what is in season, what is at my doorstep, and what I can grow in my garden. My 'garden' has grown from a few pot plants of herbs, to fruit trees and garden beds. I have always felt the need to have something growing. Even when I lived on campus at university I grew alfalfa sprouts to have fresh in my sandwiches.

I started out in town planning, fascinated by the way we humans live in cities. I worked on some great projects, some of which involved changing the landcape through food, either in urban renewal of laneways or implementing community gardens in small spaces. I always loved gardening and cooking and being creative—it's my escape, and I have decided that is where I want my life path to go.

I currently have in my garden passionfruit vines, a quince tree, a fig tree, an apricot tree, a peach tree, two apple trees, raspberries, a pomegranate tree, a kaffir lime tree, a kumquat tree, leafy greens of lettuce and herbs, broad beans, chervil, tarragon, mint, parsley, wood sorrel, fat hen, chickweed, fennel pollen, Jerusalem artichokes, asparagus (plants last for 20 years!), zucchini, beetroot, kale—oh, and thyme, lots and lots of thyme. And I can't wait for tomato and basil season!

I like to grow things that are hard to find in the shops—you just can't beat freshly picked squeaky vegetables. I also love to forage for food, picking up leaves and seeds as I go and cooking with them and also transplanting them back into my garden. I now have wild vegetables and edible weeds such as fat hen,

wild sorrel, fennel, wild garlic all growing in my garden now. I love to eat organic food, but am realistic when life gets in the way of buying it. But my garden is chemical free.

The organic and health food sections are really growing in most major supermarkets and a lot of the ingredients I use are now available there too. Wild rabbit and venison, for example, can usually be found there and can really sing when cooked with the right ingredients. Don't forget your farmers' markets—it's your next best to growing your own.

Making food from scratch takes time but is so rewarding. I love to have a stockpile of preserves, pickles, jams and chutneys. If you have a well stocked pantry you can always create something special.

It was my love of making food from scratch that prompted my boyfriend, Dan, to suggest I go on MasterChef. I had made him a Victoria sponge for his birthday and while we were eating it, he said, 'Hey Emma, you are a really good cook and I reckon you would do okay on that show.' We had been talking about the dream of one day opening a restaurant together. So I decided to give it a go. That has become my motto really, 'just give it a go'. It is working so far.

I managed to put together my written application and audition video while I was home sick with pneumonia. I must have really wanted to get on MasterChef, as I could hardly breathe making that audition video. A few weeks later I got the magic phone call and was invited to come in and audition with a prepared cold dish. I decided to make the tea-smoked salmon and homemade bread. I was called in for a second audition to cook a hot dish. I was so excited and nervous! I made a rabbit and pancetta dish. I have included these recipes in the book.

Life carried on—I was waiting for weeks when I got a phone call to say I had been shortlisted. The next minute the judges from the show—Gary Mehigan, George Calombaris and Matt Preston—knocked on my door and came into my tiny kitchen. They told me I had to do a challenge while they sat and watched me. So I did, and at the end of the meal they gave me the famous white apron, I almost fainted!

From there on in, it was a complete whirlwind and I never thought I would win it. But a part of me secretly hoped I would and just took each day as it came. I was determined to get stuck in, be myself, and have a go, and my love of cooking just shone throughout my journey.

Since the show, I have found that I cook without recipes a lot more. I used to always refer to a recipe, whereas now I can create things for myself. I am so much more confident; I will pick up anything and have a go. Lynton and I would practice a lot while we stayed in the MasterChef house and our mantra was 'just one more thing'. Before we retired for the evening, we would do just one more little technique or idea we had been thinking about. Secondly, because there was never any time to think on the show it forced me to draw on my knowledge and skills and to adapt from recipes and techniques that I knew. I encourage you to do the same. If you think a recipe would benefit from a bit of extra this or a bit less of that, then do it! Make the recipes your own.

MasterChef really allowed me to focus on what is important to me. It has helped me to develop and refine my food style and has really increased my knowledge of all things food. I can think outside the square so much more now and have an arsenal of new techniques I have learnt at my disposal. I am really grateful to the judges and the chefs who appeared on the show for their help and support.

I am proud that I grew up in Central Victoria in a beautiful town called Bendigo, and although I now live in Melbourne, I am still a country kid at heart. I want to challenge the perception of local and seasonal food—farm-gate food really means beautiful artisan food.

As well as some obviously tried and tested recipes that I have been cooking for years, I have also tried to include as many exciting, inspired new recipes that I have been working on over the past six months as I can. I hope that you will love these recipes as much as I do. xx Emma

BASIC KITCHEN EQUIPMENT

- Digital thermometer—so easy and will change your life
- Digital scales—makes cooking easy and takes the guesswork out of measuring. I use digital scales to measure liquids as well as dry goods.
- Good sharp knife and sharpening steel
- Cup measures and measuring spoons
- Non-stick frying pan
- Heavy cast-iron pan (skillet)
- Skewers for testing meat and cakes
- Dough scraper for making dough
- Silicon spatula for folding and scraping mixture out of bowls
- Pressure cooker—a really great way to reduce cooking time

Another note: all butter is unsalted, all eggs, pork and chickens are free-range, eschalots and shallots are much the same thing (little brown French onions), spring onions are the long slim green and white onions. Cook with love and you can't go wrong!

WEIGHTS AND MEASURES

British and US tablespoon measurements are 15 ml.

Metric spoon and cup measurements	Cup conversions for metric ingredient
½ teaspoon = 2.5 g	1 cup = 250 ml/9 fl oz
1 teaspoon = 5 g	½ cup = 125 ml/4 fl oz
1 teaspoon = 5 ml	⅓ cup = 165 ml/5½ fl oz
1 tablespoon = 20 ml	¼ cup = 60 ml/2 fl oz

Foraging

'Wild food is the ultimate in seasonal, local and sustainable produce'
— Miles Irving

Foraging has changed the way I look at the urban landscape. What was once perceived as a pest to be removed, is now a thing of beauty (and a potential meal). I foraged nettles near my home for the nettle pesto and pasta in this book. I foraged the wild garlic from near the beautiful Yarra River, and the saltbush and samphire from Brighton foreshore. Food surrounds us. I use foraged ingredients chiefly because they taste wonderful. Just remember, every single mass-produced fruit or vegetable you can buy on the market today started out life as a wild plant. Lots of vegetables were selectively bred for size, shape and colour and sometimes at the detriment of flavour.

Foraged wild plants are packed full of intense, punchy flavours (not to mention vitamins and minerals). These are tastes that our ancestors had been enjoying for thousands of years. Today, there is a world wide rennaisance happening towards wild food and foraging. Like many food trends it has probably been led by top chefs, restaurants and foragers—people like Rene Redzepi of Noma, or Miles Irving, author of the *Forager Handbook*, to name but a few. But unlike other trends, I hope this one is back for good.

Just a word of caution, please only forage plants that you are 100 per cent confident in identifying—especially wild mushrooms. There are numerous books available and the internet now has trusted sources you can refer to. Also, when collecting nettles, please wear gloves!

I like to garnish my salads with a few foraged leaves such as:

Chickweed – pea flavour
Wild sorrel – lemon zest
Young dandelion leaves – bitter flavour
Nasturtium flowers – sweetness
Nasturtium leaves – peppery flavour
Pineapple sage leaves – tastes of sweet pineapples
Wild garlic leaves – mild garlic flavour
Wild fennel – aniseed flavours
Wild rocket – strong peppery taste
Pig face – salty and juicy
Sea spinach – salty and refreshing
Samphire – salty and juicy
Fat hen – earthy and 'iron-y'

Good Morning

Breakfast and Brunch

Homemade breakfast can be so quick to make, and, with a bit of preparation (cracking out a homemade chutney), you can have a café-style breakfast in your own home, while still in your pyjamas! Breakfast is a time to savour homemade butter on buttermilk crumpets and freshly made jam on fruit loaf.

Sometimes I am in the garden with a coffee first thing. The garden is my main source of inspiration—my happy place. Walking back into the kitchen in my dressing gown with just-picked homegrown veggies is just so satisfying and inspiring. After all, if you have great-tasting raw produce, the cooking part is easy!

When I was growing up, we had a Jersey cow at home. I would sit next to Mum many mornings watching her milk Daisy. We were lucky to have fresh milk and cream every day. Mum would give us a jar with cream and a marble in it. It was our job to take turns and shake and shake that jar until we eventually made butter. I thought it took hours, but in reality it only takes about 30 minutes! If you have kids, I urge you to give this a try one morning, it's great fun. I have since ditched the jar and now make butter in five minutes using my mixer.

My mum made us homemade muesli when we were children and she still does. I broke away and went through a big bircher muesli stage when I lived with my sister Rachel and developed this great recipe to make at home. It's best to choose a thick Greek yoghurt to serve with it, or you can make your own.

- -

The Most Amazing Bircher Muesli Ever

250 g (9 oz) rolled oats
zest and juice of 1 orange
zest and juice of 1 lemon
2 large Granny Smith apples, coarsely grated
  with skin on
80 g (2½ oz) runny honey

250 ml (9 fl oz) thick Greek yoghurt
about half a cup each of fresh blueberries and
  poached pears or poached quinces
toasted nuts, to garnish

Weigh your oats into a plastic container or stainless steel bowl and add water until the oats are just barely covered—when you push down on the oats a puddle of water should appear.

Set aside for a minimum of 1 hour, or overnight, in the refrigerator.

Combine all the other ingredients, except the nuts, and stir into the oats.

Garnish with toasted nuts and serve.

Note: This will keep for 5 days in the refrigerator.

When Dan and I were travelling in Cambodia, we came across this great way to start the day. You can find black rice in your local Asian grocery or in some supermarkets. Don't confuse black rice with wild rice; black rice is cheaper and is a very different texture and flavour. Once cooked with coconut, milk and sugar, it becomes soft, creamy and purple. Add extra water to adjust consistency, as desired.

Black Rice Porridge

serves 2

½ cup black rice
1 x 400 ml (14 fl oz) can coconut milk
250 ml (9 fl oz) water
4 tablespoons panela sugar (cane sugar)
    or raw sugar

salt, to taste
fresh mango cheeks, sliced, to serve
shaved fresh coconut, to serve

Place the rice, coconut milk and water in a saucepan and bring to a simmer, with the lid on. Stir regularly until it is very soft and creamy (about 30 minutes).

Add sugar and salt to taste.

Serve with mango cheeks and shaved fresh coconut on top.

Good Morning

The smell of crumpets coming from the kitchen in the morning is so lovely. These are easy to cook in a pan and don't need the oven! You could also serve these with smoked salmon, crème fraîche and capers.

Homemade Buttermilk Crumpets

makes 8

150 ml (5 fl oz) Homemade Buttermilk
  (see Basics)
225 g (8 oz) strong plain (all-purpose) flour
¼ teaspoon salt
½ teaspoon white (granulated) sugar
1 teaspoon active dry yeast
150 ml (5 fl oz) warm water
¼ teaspoon bicarbonate of soda (baking soda)
1 teaspoon butter, for greasing

honey, fresh ricotta or Berry Jam, to serve
  (see Basics)

Warm the buttermilk to room temperature. Mix all the dry ingredients, except for the bicarbonate of soda, together in a large bowl. Make a well and pour in the warmed buttermilk and warm water. Mix into a batter. Cover with a tea towel or cling film and leave in a warm, draught-free place (on the kitchen bench or near a radiator).

Leave it to rise for an hour, until it has doubled in size and the mixture is light and spongy. Stir the batter to knock back any air. Now add the bicarbonate of soda and stir in well.

Transfer the batter to a pouring jug and leave in a warm place for 30 minutes.

Heat a non-stick frying pan on the stovetop over a medium-high heat. Grease four egg rings with butter. Place the egg rings in the pan and pour in enough batter to fill the rings halfway up the sides.

Cook until bubbles form on the top—about ten minutes. Lift away the rings, and flip over the crumpets. Fry for two minutes and remove. Place to one side and cook the remaining crumpets.

Serve warm with honey, ricotta or Berry Jam.

In my garden, I grow figs, quinces, apricots, peaches and raspberries. These fruits are so much better when they are homegrown and picked off the tree, warmed from the sun. When there is a glut, I dry the apricots and figs. My fig tree is called Mr Figgins and my quince tree is called Quincy Jones and I inspect them daily. They are both wonderful trees to grow as they are low maintenance.

Toasted Fruit Loaf with Tea-poached Fruit

makes 2 loaves

FRUIT LOAF
100 g (3½ oz) sultanas, chopped
100 g (3½ oz) dried apricots, chopped
100 g (3½ oz) dried figs, chopped
100 g (3½ oz) dates, chopped
2 tablespoons rum
60 g (2 oz) unsalted butter, at room temperature
250 ml (9 fl oz) full-fat milk
7 g (one sachet) dry yeast
500 g (17½ oz) strong bread flour
40 g (1½ oz) caster (superfine) sugar
2 teaspoons salt
2 large eggs, lightly beaten
125 g (4 oz) flaked almonds
2 teaspoons cinnamon

½ teaspoon allspice
zest of 2 large lemons, grated
zest of 2 large oranges, grated
butter, for greasing
1 egg, whisked, for wash
pinch of salt

TEA-POACHED FRUIT
600 ml (21 fl oz) brewed black tea (strength is how you like to drink it)
4 pears or peaches or other soft fruit
300 g (10½ oz) sugar
cinnamon stick
1 clove
½ star anise

To make the loaves, firstly soak all of the dried fruit in the rum (you may need a little more rum—add more at your discretion), for about an hour.

Add the butter to the milk and warm until the butter melts (don't heat it higher than 60°C (170°F) as this will kill the yeast).

In a large bowl, mix the yeast, flour, sugar and salt together. Blend in the warm milk mixture and then the beaten eggs. You can do this by hand, by taking the dough out of the bowl and kneading on a flour-free bench for 10–15 minutes. Alternatively, use an electric mixer with a dough hook to knead the dough for 5 minutes, and finish it by hand for a few minutes—the best of both worlds.

Toasted Fruit Loaf
with Tea-poached Fruit (cont.)

Rest the dough in the mixing bowl, in a warm place, for about 40 minutes to an hour or until the dough doubles in size.

Sprinkle the almonds on a baking tray and toast in a preheated oven at 150°C (300°F) until they are golden brown. Cool.

In a large bowl, mix in the rum-soaked fruit, nuts, spices and the citrus zest. Knead the mixture into the dough for one minute until all the fruit is evenly distributed.

Divide the dough into two equal pieces and mould each into a rough ball. Place each ball onto a tray lined with baking paper. Place a tea towel over the top and rest the dough again for 30 minutes.

For this recipe, I like to shape my loaves into oval blobs and bake them freestyle, but you can also use loaf tins. Whisk the egg wash with the pinch of salt and brush across the top of the two loaves. Cut a deep incision (at least 2 cm/1 in deep) lengthways down the middle of each loaf.

Raise the oven temperature to 200°C (400°F). Bake the two loaves for 30 minutes or until they are dark golden on top and are hollow when tapped.

To make the tea-poached fruit, firstly brew the tea. Remove the core and stone from the fruit and halve—I like to leave the skin on. Place the tea, sugar, cinnamon stick, clove and star anise in a pan and bring to the boil. Add the fruit and simmer to poach until tender (5 minutes maximum depending on the ripeness of your fruit). The fruit should be easy to pierce with a skewer.

Slice and toast the fruit loaf and serve the fruit on top, with a dollop of ricotta if you like. Keep any unused fruit in the sugar syrup. You can also serve the toast and fruit with cream.

I like to use duck eggs when I can because of their bright orange creamy yolks. You can often find them at farmers' markets. The yolk is very rich and, with the addition of cream and lashings of butter, make a wonderfully indulgent breakfast. Your breakfast friends will beat down your door for this one.

Scrambled Duck Eggs with Smoked Salmon on Homemade Bread

4 servings Double Tea-smoked Salmon (see Basics) (or 400 g/14 oz smoked salmon)
8 duck eggs (2 per person or you can just use chicken eggs if you can't find duck eggs)
100 ml (3½ fl oz) fresh thickened cream
2 big knobs of butter, for frying and for
buttering the toast
sea salt and freshly cracked black pepper, to season
4 slices Easy Awesome Bread (see Basics)
Homemade Butter (see Basics), to serve

Finely slice the smoked salmon into strips.

Whisk the eggs and cream together. Heat a non-stick pan over a high heat, and melt 1 knob of butter. Season the egg mixture and pour it into the pan. Fold the eggs quickly as they cook. Just before the eggs are set, fold in the salmon pieces for about 5 seconds and then remove from pan.

Slice and toast the bread and spread with lashings of butter. Serve the eggs on the side.

You can buy wild mushrooms in markets and supermarkets, or there are courses on how to forage for wild mushrooms, with experienced guides (do not eat a mushroom you aren't sure of—mushrooms can be deadly). I like Pine Mushrooms, Slippery Jacks (a member of the Cep/ Porcini family—the king of mushrooms) and King Browns. Never wash mushrooms—use a pastry brush to remove any random bits of debris.

Wild garlic leaves are the green part of the garlic plant. They add a beautiful colour and a mild garlic flavour. They are easily foraged during springtime. You can also make this recipe with horseradish leaves.

Wild Mushrooms with Bacon and Wild Garlic Leaves on Toast

4 slices Dry-cured Bacon (see Basics)
3 tablespoons butter, plus extra butter to spread
150 g (5 oz) wild mushrooms or a selection of
   mushrooms
3–4 long garlic leaves (or horseradish leaves),
   roughly chopped

2 chunky slices Easy Awesome Bread
   (see Basics)
freshly cracked black pepper, to taste

Fry the bacon in a non-stick pan over a high heat until it is crispy. Set aside.

Add 2 tablespoons of the butter to the pan. Brush the mushrooms clean of any debris and slice them lengthways. Sauté the mushrooms in the butter and bacon fat for 4 to 5 minutes. Add the garlic leaves and sauté for another minute.

Heat a griddle pan and char-grill chunky slices of bread. Spread the remaining butter on the bread. Pile the mushrooms and garlic leaves on the bread, place the crispy bacon on top and then some freshly cracked pepper.

You could also serve this with a simple poached egg (see Egg Hints and Tips on page 40).

A Homegrown Table

I love growing heirloom tomatoes in my garden because they look fabulous and taste how tomatoes should taste. I often forget how good this combination is on toast, so I have put it in here as a little reminder for a very quick, easy breakfast.

Avocado and Feta Smash on Toast with Heirloom Tomatoes

1 ripe avocado
½ lemon, juiced
sea salt and freshly cracked pepper, to taste
100 g (3½ oz) Persian feta cheese, crumbled
250 g (9 oz) small heirloom tomatoes of
*   different colours (medley) or 1 big tomato*
*   (such as a Black Krim)*

2 slices Easy Awesome Bread (see Basics)
basil leaves, torn, to garnish
extra virgin olive oil, to garnish
lemon wedges, to serve

Remove the stone and skin from avocado and chop roughly. In a bowl, add the avocado and lemon juice and season with salt and pepper. Mix gently.

Crumble the feta cheese and season with salt and pepper.

Slice or quarter the tomatoes, depending on their size.

Toast the bread slices.

To serve, dollop the avocado mixture onto the toast slices, sprinkle with feta cheese and top with the fresh tomatoes.

Garnish with basil leaves and a drizzle of olive oil and squeeze of lemon

Breakfast doesn't have to be sweet; these croquettes are delicious and crunchy and can be made with any white fish. Prepare the fish mixture the night before and you have a quick and tasty brunch. I love 'em.

Salt Cod Croquettes and Oven-roasted Tomatoes

serves 4

SALT COD CROQUETTES

2 tablespoons coarse sea salt

500 g (17½ oz) fillet white flesh fish (such as cod or whiting)

4 medium-sized Dutch creams or Maris piper potatoes (about 600 g/21 oz), peeled

2 cups full-fat or skim milk, for poaching

2 handfuls flat-leaf parsley leaves, chopped

sea salt and freshly cracked black pepper, to taste

½ cup plain (all-purpose) flour

4 eggs, lightly whisked

1 cup breadcrumbs (I prefer Panko), to coat

500 ml (1 pint) vegetable oil, for frying

OVEN-ROASTED TOMATOES

250 g (9 oz) cherry plum tomatoes

2 tablespoons olive oil

2 eschallots, peeled and sliced

1 clove garlic, crushed

sprigs of your choice of rosemary, thyme, basil and oregano

sea salt and freshly cracked black pepper, to taste

1 teaspoon sugar

To make the croquettes, place the fish on a plate and rub in the sea salt. Cover with cling film and place the plate in the refrigerator overnight.

Preheat the oven to 150°C (300°F).

To roast the tomatoes, place them in an oven tray with the oil, eschalots, garlic, rosemary, thyme, basil or oregano, salt, pepper and sugar. Roast for about 20 minutes.

Meanwhile, boil the potatoes until they are very soft. Strain and mix in a large bowl and set aside. The mix does not have to be perfectly smooth, in fact a few lumps add a bit of texture to the final croquette.

A Homegrown Table

Salt Cod Croquettes and Oven-roasted Tomatoes (cont.)

Wash the salt off the fish. In a flat deep pan, pour in the milk and lay the fish fillet in the milk. Bring to the boil and simmer gently for 5 minutes until the fish is cooked. Strain.

Crumble the fish into the mashed potatoes. Add the chopped parsley. Season with salt and pepper and mash together.

Sprinkle the flour on a plate or board. Place the eggs in a small bowl and whisk lightly. Add the breadcrumbs in another bowl. Portion the mash into thumb-length logs and roll in flour, dip into the beaten egg and then dip into the breadcrumbs.

Heat the vegetable oil to 180°C (350°F) in a deep saucepan or fryer.

When the oil is ready for frying, drop in the croquettes and deep-fry until golden brown—approximately 1–2 minutes. Remove them with a slotted spoon and place on kitchen paper to drain. Serve with the oven-roasted tomatoes.

A Homegrown Table

I have chickens in my backyard and I love them. I feed them all of the food scraps and they repay you with beautiful fresh eggs. Chooks are great at keeping the snails at bay.

My mum loves this breakfast. Serve this in individual ramekins, copper pots like I have or all together in one dish.

Baked Farm Eggs with Wild Mushrooms, Spinach and Parmesan

2 knobs butter
250 g (9 oz) wild mushrooms
½ bunch English spinach leaves
1 clove garlic, to taste
salt and pepper, to taste
150 g (5 oz) thickened cream

4 eggs
4 large shaves parmesan (about 35 g/1¼ oz)
4 tablespoons Tomato Kasundi (optional, see Basics)

Preheat the oven to 190°C (375°F).

In a deep frying pan, heat the butter and sauté the wild mushrooms with the spinach. Pierce the garlic clove with your fork and use the fork to stir in the mushrooms and spinach together, to give a hint of garlic. Cook until wilted and season to taste.

Splash in the cream.

Pour the mixture into individual ovenproof pans or ramekins or across the bottom of one ovenproof dish. Crack the eggs on top. Bake for 10 minutes or until the egg white is cooked and the yolk is still runny. You may have to watch this carefully so it doesn't overcook.

Once they are ready, remove the ramekins from the oven and add the parmesan shaves over each egg. Serve with a dollop of tomato kasundi on top.

Egg Hints and Tips

Poached Eggs

*I love a good poached egg and they are easy to make with these neat tips.
Boil the water in a deep saucepan. Add about 2 tablespoons of vinegar (I usually use white wine vinegar, but have been known to use whatever is in the cupboard).
Once the water has boiled, reduce the heat to low. Using a slotted spoon, swirl the water around the saucepan in a whirlpool. Crack your fresh eggs one at a time into a cup and then pour one at a time into the whirlpool.
Poach to your liking—I like mine with just a bit of wobble, which only takes a few minutes.*

Scrambled Eggs

*Before you start, you will need your toast ready to go on a plate.
Lightly whisk together 3 whole eggs and 60 ml (2 fl oz) of thickened cream (35% fat). Season with salt and pepper and then set aside.
Preheat your best non-stick pan until hot.
Add a knob of butter to the pan, quickly followed by your eggs. Mix using a heatproof rubber spatula.
Stir the egg mixture vigorously. You are looking to create moist soft pieces of egg—not a fine bobbly texture. Aim to pour the eggs from the hot pan just before they are ready as they will be hot and continue to cook. Serve on hot buttered toast!*

Midday

Light Meals and Starters

These meals are perfect in the middle of the day. Some of them are quick to prepare, while others require a bit more time. I especially enjoy making lunch for friends on the weekend and, when the weather is warm and the sun is out, we often eat in the garden.

Fresh produce from the garden, and the occasional foraged ingredient, is the basis for many of these meals—don't be afraid to make your meals seasonally driven. Have a look at what is in your garden or at your local market and dress the dish to the seasons. I have included my favourite soup recipes—they are so quick and easy and great to showcase one vegetable, like celeriac, or my favourite Jerusalem artichoke, or even chestnuts. Make sure you enjoy the soups with some homemade bread.

Tips for cooking vegetables

If it grows under the ground, start it off in salted cold water.
If it grows above the ground, put it straight into boiling water.

These are marvellous. So tasty and delicious with a glass of white wine. They are quick enough to prepare for unexpected visitors.

- -

Blue Cheese Puffs

serves 4–6

250 ml (9 fl oz) cold water
100 g (3½ oz) unsalted butter, chopped
pinch of salt
140 g (5 oz) plain (all-purpose) flour, sifted
4 eggs
80 g (2½ oz) firm blue cheese, crumbled
black pepper, to taste
flaked sea salt, to serve

Preheat the oven to 200°C (400°F).

Combine the water, butter and salt in a saucepan over a medium heat until the butter is melted. Bring to the boil then turn the heat down very low. Using a wooden spoon, mix in the flour until one big ball forms. Remove from the heat and put the mixture into an electric mixer and leave to cool a little. Beat the dough, adding the eggs one at a time, until it is smooth and glossy. Fold in the cheese and cracked black pepper to taste and mix in gently.

Spoon teaspoon-sized balls onto a baking paper–lined baking tray. Bake for 10 minutes. Turn the oven down to 180°C (350°F) and bake for a further 8–10 minutes until golden and puffed.

Remove from the oven and sprinkle them with flaked sea salt.

This is an absolute ripper. Potatoes are easy to grow in the ground, or you can get a growing kit from your local nursery. I learnt this recipe from my brother-in-law, Richard, who learnt it from his father. It really showcases the dill and potatoes in their brilliant simplicity.

- -

Dill, Potato and Wild Sorrel Salad

serves 4, as a side dish

8–12 Kipfler potatoes
1 clove garlic
1 teaspoon sea salt, plus extra to taste
200 ml (7 fl oz) natural Greek yoghurt
100 ml (3½ fl oz) Homemade Mayonnaise
    (see Basics)
1 bunch dill leaves, chopped
1 handful wild sorrel leaves, leaves left whole
    so you can appreciate their beauty

Wash and cover the potatoes, unskinned, in salted cold water and bring to the boil. Simmer gently until just cooked, firm rather than soft.

With a mortar and pestle, mash the clove of garlic and salt and grind them together.

Mix the Greek yoghurt and mayonnaise together and combine with the garlic and salt. Add more salt to taste. Mix the dill leaves into the yoghurt mixture. The yoghurt mixture should taste almost too salty—but this is okay as the potatoes will balance it all out.

Drain and remove the potatoes and cool slightly. Leave the skins on and slice into 2 cm (¾ in) lengths. Fold the potatoes into the yoghurt mixture.

Serve with a garnish of wild sorrel leaves for a nice lemony punch.

Midday

I forage samphire or coastal spinach leaves along the coast. Foraged sea herbs respond well to a quick pickling or eat them in their fresh unadulterated state. This dish is great served with champagne in the garden.

Double Tea-smoked Salmon with Pickled Cucumber, Sea Herbs and Crème Fraîche

4 servings Double Tea-smoked Salmon
   (see Basics), or 400 g (14 oz) smoked
   salmon)
1 serving Pickled Cucumber (see Basics)
handful of coastal spinach/samphire leaves
2–4 cm (1–2 in) fresh horseradish root, grated

½ cup crème fraîche
1 tablespoon extra virgin olive oil, to serve

Make the Pickled Cucumber, following the recipe, but don't drain.

Add the coastal spinach/samphire leaves to the pickling liquid for 5 minutes, then drain the pickled cucumber and greens.

In a bowl, add the horseradish root to the crème fraîche and mix.

Arrange the salmon, greens and crème fraîche on a platter and drizzle with extra virgin olive oil.

Serve with fresh bread and Homemade Butter (see Basics).

I made this dish when Chef Matt Germanchis worked with me as my mentor. Under his guidance, I was able to refine this dish, which impressed the judges so much I was one of the top dishes of the day. I love that this dish is a dish unto itself—all the seasoning is in the olive brine.

Butter-poached Fish with Leek and Fennel

serves 4

1 x 250 ml (9 fl oz) jar green olives in brine
1 leek
1 fennel bulb, with fronds
1 cup chicken stock
1 cup water
1 cup Beurre Noisette (see Basics)

500 g (17½ oz) white fish fillets,
   such as John Dory
150 g (5 oz) butter plus extra 2 tablespoons
rosemary flowers, to garnish
pale inside leaves of celery, to garnish

Preheat the oven to 180°C (350°F).

Take out 12 olives from the jar and slice the cheeks off the stone. Set to one side. You will also need about half a cup of brine.

Trim the top green top off the leek, leaving the white end, which you will use for this recipe.

Cut off the fronds of the fennel bulb and slice the fennel bulb segments into leaf shapes. Line an oven tray with baking paper and sprinkle the fronds on top. Bake in the oven for about 10–20 minutes, until they are burnt.

In a saucepan on a low heat, combine the chicken stock and water with ½ cup of the olive brine—and add more brine or water according to taste. Add the fennel bulb segments and the whole white part of the leek and simmer gently until soft—for no more than 10 minutes.

Butter-poached Fish
with Leek and Fennel (cont.)

In the meantime, pour the beurre noisette into a sous vide bag or a zip lock bag, and place in the fish fillets, trying not to overlap the fish fillets. Heat the water to 58°C (136°F) and maintain that temperature for 15 minutes. You can use a water bath or a saucepan with water and a thermometer. I use a saucepan with a thermometer at home and it works just fine. Heat the water to 58°C (136°F) and then turn the heat off. Check every few minutes and when the temperature starts to drop, turn the heat back on until the water reaches 58°C (136°F) again. The fish should be cooked after 15 minutes. If so, remove it from the water bath and set aside. If you are using a thick piece of fish you may need to cook it for a little longer (this length of time is for a John Dory fillet).

Remove all the green vegetables from the poaching liquid and set the liquid aside. Char-grill the whole leek on a griddle pan on each side to create nice brown lines and then slice the leek across into pinwheels or just slice into rounds.

Melt 150 g (5 oz) of the butter into 1 cup of the poaching liquid and whisk to a light buttery sauce.

Remove the fish from the sous vide bag and discard the beurre noisette. Tear the fillets into rough pieces.

To serve, place 3-4 slices of leek onto a plate, with 3–4 fennel petals and the olive slices. Place the fish pieces on top and sprinkle with the burnt fennel fronds. Drizzle over the butter sauce. Garnish with rosemary flowers and the inside pale leaves of celery.

This is a dish I made to celebrate all the natural earthy flavours of foraging. Nasturtium leaves grow everywhere and have a wonderful fresh, peppery taste.

A Foraged Plate

Steak Tartare with Artichoke Chips and Nasturtium Leaves

450 g (15 oz) whole beef eye fillet, trimmed of sinew and fat
500 ml (17½ fl oz/2 cups) chicken stock
2 cups picked tarragon leaves
2 eschalots, 1 peeled and chopped, the other sliced very thinly into rings
1½ tablespoons apple balsamic vinegar (optional)
3 teaspoons apple cider vinegar
200 ml (7 fl oz) grapeseed oil
2 tablespoons Dijon mustard
4 eggs
¼ teaspoon ground nutmeg
¼ teaspoon ground cinnamon
¼ teaspoon ground ginger

¼ teaspoon ground cloves
½ teaspoon ground white pepper
200 ml (7 fl oz) thickened cream
1 tablespoon sherry vinegar
3 tablespoons juniper berries
1 teaspoon caraway seeds
1 tablespoon butter
2 thin slices rye bread
6 Jerusalem artichokes
salt and pepper, to taste
2 cups vegetable oil, to deep-fry
olive oil, to drizzle
1 teaspoon finely grated horseradish
2 handfuls nasturtium leaves, to garnish

Place the beef on a chopping board. Using a very sharp knife, scrape the fillet gently with the edge of the knife. This will produce a lovely textural tartare without it being 'mincey'. Set aside until needed.

Place the stock in a saucepan and bring to the boil over high heat. Cook for 25 minutes or until reduced to about 50 ml (1¾ fl oz).

To make the tarragon sauce, place the tarragon, eschalot, garlic, apple balsamic vinegar, cider vinegar and reduced chicken stock into a blender, and process for 30 seconds until the herbs are finely chopped. With the motor running, slowly add 160 ml (5½ fl oz) grapeseed oil and process for about 3 minutes until thick and emulsified. Season with salt. Strain through a fine sieve into a bowl, then refrigerate until needed.

A Foraged Plate (cont.)
Steak Tartare with Artichoke Chips and Nasturtium Leaves

- -

To make Dijon oil, whisk Dijon mustard and the remaining 2 tablespoons of grapeseed oil in a small bowl until well combined. Set aside.

Heat some water in a saucepan to 62°C (144°F). Place the eggs into the water and cook at this temperature for 45 minutes. Remove the eggs with a slotted spoon, cool, and very carefully, peel eggs and separate the yolks. Set aside the yolks.

Preheat the oven to 160°C (320°F).

Combine the nutmeg, cinnamon, ginger, cloves and white pepper in a small bowl and set aside. Beat cream in a bowl until soft peaks form, then fold in the mixed spices and sherry vinegar until just combined. Set aside.

In a small frying pan, toast the juniper berries until fragrant, then add the caraway seeds and continue to toast until fragrant. Remove from the heat and pound the toasted juniper berries and caraway seeds in a mortar and pestle until finely ground.

Melt the butter in a small frying pan set over medium heat. Fry the rye bread for 1–2 minutes each side until golden. Remove the bread, then crumble it when it is cool enough to handle. Set aside.

Scrub the artichokes well and thinly slice them. Deep fry in vegetable oil at 180°C (350°F) until they float and are crispy.

To serve, divide the beef among plates, and season to taste with salt and pepper. Drizzle over the Dijon oil and tarragon sauce, scatter with thinly sliced eschalot, horseradish and the rye bread crumble. Spoon a dollop of spiced cream to the side, and place one of the egg yolks in the centre (to look like a cracked egg). Garnish with artichoke chips and nasturtium leaves, and sprinkle with the juniper berry mixture.

I used to be afraid to cook duck, but I find that this way of cooking duck breast is fail-safe. Remember that duck breast should still be pink when cooked.

Crispy Skin Duck, to Match the Seasons

SUMMER (PICTURED)
½ fennel bulb
½ blood orange
Basic Vinaigrette (see Basics)
pineapple sage flowers

WINTER
2 eschalots (shallots)
2 tablespoons olive oil
1 clove garlic
½ carrot, finely diced
½ celery stick, finely diced
½ cup puy lentils
1½ cups Brown Chicken Stock (see Basics)
splash of white wine

2 sprigs thyme
salt and pepper, to taste

SAUCE
1 tablespoon caster (superfine) sugar
2 tablespoons red wine vinegar
zest and juice of ½ lemon
zest and juice of 2 oranges
1 cup Brown Chicken Stock (see Basics)
salt and pepper, to taste
pomegranate seeds or pineapple sage flowers, to garnish

2 duck breasts

Summer

Remove the top and finely slice the fennel bulb lengthways, and cleanly peel the orange with a knife and cut the orange into small segments. Toss together.

Lightly dress the salad with the vinaigrette.

Winter

Sauté the eschalots in the olive oil until translucent. Add the garlic, carrot and celery and sauté for another minute. Add the lentils, stock, white wine and thyme, and simmer for 30 minutes until the lentils are cooked. Season with salt and pepper. Remove the thyme stalks.

Crispy Skin Duck, to Match the Seasons (cont.)

Sauce

In a saucepan, dissolve the sugar and vinegar over a low heat and cook until the liquid turns a deep golden caramel colour. Pour in the citrus juices and stock. Bring to the boil and simmer gently for 30 minutes. Skim the surface as necessary. The mixture is ready when it thickens and coats the back of a spoon.

Pass the sauce through a sieve and season with salt and pepper. Add the drained zest.

Heat a non-stick saucepan to a medium heat. Place the breasts skin-side down and pan-sear for 8–10 minutes or until the skin is crispy. Drain the fat off as it renders down and set aside for other uses (such as crispy potatoes, see page 158).

Once the skin is crispy, flip the duck breast over, so the skin is facing upwards, and cook for another 2 minutes. Remove from the heat and rest the duck.

To serve, place a portion of the salad or lentils on each plate, slice the duck on an angle and arrange to the side. Drizzle the sauce over the top. Garnish with pomegranate seeds or pineapple sage flowers.

Midday

Jerusalem artichokes grow really easily. They need very little care and they grow equally well in a pot. Just plant them like potatoes and watch the harvest. Don't put the peelings in the compost heap or they will start growing! This is quite a strong soup so you don't need to serve much—it is lovely as a starter. It has a beautiful creamy consistency and I like to serve it in tea cups with a sprinkle of freshly grated nutmeg.

- -

Jerusalem Artichoke Soup with Nutmeg

serves 4

600 g (21 oz) Jerusalem artichokes (makes 300 g (10½ oz) once you've peeled and chopped them)
1 tablespoon butter
3 cups full-fat milk
½ teaspoon each salt and pepper
freshly grated nutmeg, to serve

Wash and peel the artichokes. Slice finely—work quickly or they will discolour. Sauté in butter in a medium saucepan, over a medium-high heat.

Pour in the milk and season with salt. Bring to a simmer and slowly cook until the artichokes are soft. Strain the artichokes, reserving the liquid.

Place the artichokes into a food processor and blend until smooth, adding in the cooking liquid, to achieve a desired consistency. Season with salt and pepper. Pour into the tea cups while still warm. Serve with some freshly grated nutmeg on top.

These are just your ordinary stinging nettles; they grow everywhere and anywhere. Nettles are so delicious that you can leave out the potato and broad beans and this soup will still taste wonderful. Be careful to use gloves and scissors when you pick nettles to prevent their irritating sting.

Nettle and Broadbean Soup

serves 4

2 eschalots (shallots), peeled, thinly sliced
1 clove garlic, thinly sliced
1 tablespoon butter
1 medium-sized potato, peeled and roughly diced
1½ litres (52 fl oz) Ham Hock Stock (see Basics)
150 g (5 oz) broad beans, shelled and double peeled (pod and oyster shell off the little bean)

1 bunch nettles (or spinach if you can't find nettles)
salt and pepper, to taste
2 thick slices Dry-cured Bacon (see Basics), diced and fried (optional)
crusty bread, to serve
croutons, to serve
shaved parmesan, to serve

In a soup pot, sauté the eschalots and garlic in the butter over a medium-high heat. Add the potato and sauté for a few minutes. Pour in the stock and bring to the boil.

Simmer until the potato is tender, or for about 15 minutes. Add in the broad beans and simmer for 5 minutes. Using gloves, remove the nettle leaves from the stalks. Add the nettle leaves to the soup mixture. Season with salt and pepper and simmer for further 5–10 minutes until the broad beans are tender.

Transfer to a food processor and blend well until smooth. Check the seasoning.

Sprinkle with the fried bacon, if using, and serve with crusty bread, crunchy croutons and shaved parmesan.

You could also stir through some pulled ham reserved from the ham hock stock and mix it through the nettle soup as a modern take on pea and ham soup.

This soup brings an earthiness to your kitchen. You can leave out the truffle and it will still taste delicious!

- -

Celeriac, Chervil and Truffle Soup

1 large celeriac
1 eschalot (shallot), peeled and sliced
2 tablespoons olive oil
1½ cups water
1½ cups full-fat milk
4 tablespoons cream
salt and black pepper to taste

¼ lemon, squeezed, to serve
handful chervil leaves, to serve
fresh black truffle, to serve

Peel and chop the celeriac into cubes and discard the tops. In a large saucepan, sauté the eschalot in olive oil with the celeriac. Add water and milk and bring to the boil. Simmer until the celariac is soft.

Transfer the mixture to a food processor and blend until smooth. Add the cream, 1 tablespoon at a time, while blending. Season with salt and pepper and freshly squeezed lemon juice.

Pour into bowls. Sprinkle with freshly picked chervil leaves or a few shavings of truffle.

This is a great starter or side dish. It is perfect with a cold beer in the summer after a day spent outdoors. It also works well with crispy potato skins (see page 178).

- -

Char-grilled Vegetables with Nettle Pesto

serves 4

1 cup tightly packed nettle leaves
½ cup extra virgin olive oil
1–2 garlic cloves
60 g (2 oz) grana padano parmesan cheese,
   grated

30 g (1 oz) pine nuts or almonds
½–1 teaspoon salt
mixed slices of eggplant (aubergine), zucchini
   (courgette) and capsicum (bell pepper)

Wear gloves to pick the nettles off the stalks. Sauté the nettles, on a low heat in 1/4 cup of the olive oil until wilted—about 2–4 minutes. After this time, the sting will be well and truly gone. Remove from the heat and allow to cool.

In a food processor, blend the nettles, garlic, cheese, pine nuts, remaining olive oil and salt. Place the mixture in a small bowl.

Slice the vegetables lengthways and brush with olive oil. Char-grill on a barbecue or grill pan.

To serve, season the grilled vegetables with salt and smear with the nettle pesto. Yumbo!

This also works well with basil, nasturtium or parsley. If using one of these to make a pesto, don't sauté them first, just blend them raw with the rest of the pesto ingredients.

It is best to eat pesto on the day it is made, although it does keep for about five days in the refrigerator.

Middle Eastern food is incredible, flavoursome and fresh! My sister Rachel and I often cook this food and I have taken a lot of my recipe inspiration from her. This is a large spread and can be served with everything scattered onto platters so everyone gets a chance to try a little of everything. Use 2 whole chickens, which are then crowned. That is, the legs and thighs are removed for the honey spiced chicken, and the crowns (the breast on the bone) are used for the citrus chicken.

Middle Eastern Mezze

YOGHURT FLAT BREAD
250 ml (9 fl oz) Greek yoghurt
250 g (9 oz) self-raising (self-rising) flour
½ teaspoon baking powder (baking soda)
½ teaspoon salt

SMOKED EGGPLANT (AUBERGINE) DIP
¾ cup thick drained natural yoghurt
½ bulb garlic
olive oil, for roasting
2 large eggplants (aubergines)
2 tablespoons tahini
juice of one lemon, to taste
salt, to taste

HUMMUS
1 x 440 g (15 oz) can chickpeas
1 tablespoon tahini
1 clove garlic, finely chopped
juice of one lemon, to taste
salt, to taste

Yoghurt Flat Bread
Combine all the ingredients together in a bowl, then turn out and knead into a soft ball. Depending on the type of yoghurt, you may need to add more flour, a dusting at a time.

Divide into six portions. On a floured surface, roll out the six portions into flat discs. I like them to be wonky shaped as it adds to the fun of the dish.

Heat a griddle pan over a very high heat and cook the breads for about 30 seconds each side—they should begin to puff a little. Remove and set aside.

Smoked Eggplant (Aubergine) Dip
Line a sieve with a muslin cloth. Pour the natural yoghurt into the sieve and sit it on top of a bowl. Set aside until needed. You can do this overnight, but I find that even 30 minutes to an hour is enough. You will be left with ½ a cup.

Preheat the oven to 180°C (350°F). Place the garlic, in its skin, on a baking tray and drench in a good glug of oil. Roast the garlic until soft—for about 30 minutes.

Using an open gas flame on your stovetop, burn the skin of the eggplants as evenly as you can, using tongs to turn them. You want the skin to burn a lot, which will result in a lovely smoky flavour. Alternatively, you can grill the eggplant until the skin is black. Once burned and fairly soft inside, put the eggplants into a plastic bag to sweat, making it easier to remove the skin. Once cool, remove the burnt skin, but don't worry if a few flecks remain: this will add to the lovely smoky flavour.

SAFFRON RICE
175 g (6 oz) *basmati rice*
20 g (²/₃ oz) *butter*
1 tablespoon vegetable oil
1 onion, finely chopped
430 ml (15 fl oz) chicken stock
2 dried lemons or limes, halved or
   ¼ preserved lemons
1 large pinch saffron

HONEY GINGER-SPICED CHICKEN
1 tablespoon cumin seeds, toasted
   and ground
1 tablespoon coriander seeds,
   toasted and ground
1 teaspoon ground cinnamon
1 teaspoon ground ginger
½ teaspoon cayenne pepper
½ teaspoon smoked paprika
1 teaspoon salt
2 tablespoons olive oil
3 tablespoons honey
juice of 1 lemon
4 chicken legs
4 chicken thighs
250 g (9 oz) pitted dates
1 tablespoon pomegranate molasses

Put the flesh into a food processor and blend. Add the tahini and squeeze the garlic out of its skins. Start off with 4 cloves and add more if you want a more garlicky dip. Blend in ½ cup of strained yoghurt. Season with lemon juice and salt. Delicious!

Hummus
Drain the chickpeas from the can and add to a saucepan. Cover with fresh water and add 2 large pinches of salt. Bring the water to the boil. Simmer for 15 minutes until the chickpeas are soft. This makes all the difference to a lovely smooth hummus.

Strain the chickpeas, reserving some of the liquid, and place the chickpeas into a food processor. Blend until smooth, adding a small amount of cooking liquid if needed to loosen up the mixture. Add in the tahini and garlic and blend. Season with lemon juice and salt.

Saffron Rice
Soak the rice in water for 30 minutes.

After 25 minutes, heat the butter and oil in a saucepan over medium heat. Cook the onion for about 2–3 minutes or until translucent. Drain the rice and stir it into the onion mixture to coat.

Add 375 ml (13 fl oz/1½ cups) of the chicken stock, dried or preserved lemons and saffron to the rice. Bring to the boil, then reduce heat to low, cover and cook for about 10 minutes or until the rice is tender. Turn off the heat, and set aside to stand for 5–10 minutes.

Meanwhile, pour the remaining 60 ml (2 fl oz/¼ cup) of stock into a small saucepan set over medium heat and pour over the cooked resting rice. Fluff with a fork before serving. Keep warm until needed. Transfer one-third of the cooked rice to the saucepan with the saffron stock and stir to coat. Transfer the saffron rice to the pan with the cooked rice and stir to combine. Keep warm until needed.

CITRUS CHICKEN AND BARBERRIES WITH
SUMAC
½ cup barberries (available from Persian
grocers) or cranberries
40 g butter, softened
2 chicken crowns
olive oil, for drizzling
salt, to taste
1 lemon, halved
1 teaspoon sumac (Middle Eastern spice)

FATTOUSH
3 tomatoes, chopped
2 Lebanese cucumbers, chopped
¼ cup red seedless grapes, halved
½ bunch spring onions (scallions),
thinly sliced
3 radishes, chopped
½ small bunch purslane, chopped
½ cup mint leaves, roughly chopped
½ cup parsley leaves, roughly chopped
1 pomegranate, seeds removed
1 tablespoon sumac (Middle Eastern
spice)
1 teaspoon salt
1 tablespoon olive oil
1 Yoghurt Flat Bread (see recipe above)
or store-bought pita bread
olive oil, to drizzle
lemon juice, to drizzle
salt, to taste

Honey Ginger-spiced Chicken

Preheat the oven to 180°C (350°F).

Place dry spices, salt, oil, 2 tablespoons of the honey and lemon juice in a bowl and stir well to combine. Place chicken legs and thighs in a large roasting pan, then drizzle with the spice mixture and toss to coat. Scatter with dates and roast in the oven for 45 minutes, or until cooked through, basting every 15 minutes.

Combine remaining honey and the pomegranate molasses in a bowl. Once the chicken is cooked, glaze with the honey mixture. Keep warm until needed. This smells so delicious, it will fill your kitchen with an incredible aroma.

Citrus Chicken and Barberries with Sumac

Preheat the oven to 180°C (350°F).

Soak the barberries in boiling water for 5 minutes, drain well in a sieve and transfer to a bowl.

Mix with butter until well combined. Stuff the mixture under the skin of the chicken crowns. Roast in the oven for about 45 minutes or until cooked through. To test if a chicken is cooked, the juices should run clear if pierced with a skewer into the thickest part of the meat.

Fattoush

Preheat the oven to 180°C (350°F).

Combine the tomatoes, cucumbers, grapes, spring onions, radishes, purslane, mint and parsley and most of the pomegranate seeds in a serving bowl. Cover and refrigerate until needed.

Combine sumac, salt and olive oil in a bowl and brush well onto a large piece of yoghurt flat bread or a large pita bread. Place on a tray and toast in the oven for 12 minutes or until crisp. Remove and break into pieces. Drizzle the salad with the extra olive oil, lemon juice and salt to taste, and toss with broken flat bread to combine

Midday

Middle Eastern Mezze (cont.)

WATERMELON

*800 g (28 oz) watermelon, cut into
1 cm (⅓ in) thick slices, skin
removed*

1 tablespoon rosewater

80 g (2½ oz) halva, crumbled

¼ cup mint leaves, roughly chopped

TO SERVE

½ cup coriander (cilantro) leaves

30 g (1 oz) pistachios, toasted

*40 g (1½ oz) slivered almonds,
toasted*

Watermelon

This is a delicious fragrant snack to enjoy throughout the summer months and so easy to prepare.

Place the watermelon on a large platter or flat serving plate. Drizzle with rosewater and sprinkle with the halva and mint.

To Serve

Place saffron rice onto a large platter and top with the honey spiced and citrus chicken. Place the hummus and smoky eggplant dip in a small bowl on one side and place fattoush to the other side. Cut yoghurt flat breads into various shapes. Scatter the whole table with pomegranate seeds, coriander leaves, toasted pistchio and slivered almonds. Finish the meal with rosewater watermelon. Bliss.

I love growing salad greens! They perish so easily when you buy them, so when you grow them yourself you will always have them fresh at your fingertips. I like to grow a mixture of endive or frisée, cos and butter lettuce, rocket (arugula) and baby spinach. I like to garnish my salads with a few foraged leaves as well (see the Foraging section page 12).

Wild Green Salad

serves 4 as a side

*mixture of salad and foraged leaves (about
    4 handfuls is good for 4 people, as a side)
1 serving Basic Vinaigrette (see Basics)
2 tablespoons olive oil
4 slices Easy Awesome Bread (see Basics)
1 clove garlic*

Mix up the green leaves in a bowl and dress with the vinaigrette.

Slice the bread thinly and rub a cut garlic clove over it. Brush with olive oil. Cut into cubes and toast in the oven at 200°C (400°F) until crisp, between 5 and 10 minutes. Cool.

Top the salad with the croutons and garnish with wild/foraged leaves.

Kale is a super food! It's been called a 'nutritional powerhouse' and is so easy to grow. It also looks magnificent in the garden. This is a fabulous lunch but could be eaten any time of the day.

- -

Kale, Dry-cured Bacon and 62° Egg

serves 4

4 eggs, in shell
4 thick slices Dry-cured Bacon (see Basics)
1 large bunch kale leaves, coarsely chopped
salt and pepper, to taste
Tomato Kasundi (see Basics), to serve

Place eggs in shell in a water bath set at 62°C (144°F) and let sit at 62°C (144°F) for 45 minutes.

Slice the homemade bacon into 3 cm (1 in) lengths. Fry the bacon until it is crispy. Remove and set aside. Add the kale and sauté in bacon fat until just wilted. Season with salt and pepper.

Arrange kale and bacon onto a plate. After 45 minutes, remove the eggs from the water bath. Crack the eggs open like you would if you were cracking them raw, just be a little more gentle.

Serve warm, with tomato kasundi if desired.

I couldn't have created this recipe without the help of Lynton and Christina in the Josie Bones service challenge. Using such great flavours and ingredients, like heirloom vegetables and barley, we worked together to create this winning dish. I love the root to tip approach in cooking and in this dish I have roasted the beets, pickled their stems and used their leaves as a salad. If your beets don't come with nice leaves, any salad leaves will do.

- -

Heirloom Root Vegetables with Barley and Goat's Cheese

1 serving Vegetable Stock (see Basics)
200 g (7 oz/1 cup) barley, soaked in water for 30 minutes, drained
salt and pepper, to taste
20 (about 600 g/21 oz) baby beetroot, with leaves
180 ml (6 fl oz/¾ cup) extra virgin olive oil, plus extra to drizzle
2 teaspoons sherry vinegar
12 (about 200 g/7 oz) baby carrots, trimmed
20 g (⅔ oz) butter, chopped
60 ml (2 fl oz/¼ cup) honey

60 ml (2 fl oz/¼ cup) champagne or white wine vinegar
100 g (2½ oz) thick Greek yoghurt
2 cups rocket leaves, chopped
60 g (2 oz) pine nuts, toasted
60 g (2 oz) parmesan cheese
30 g (1 oz/¼ cup) blanched almonds, toasted
1 teaspoon cumin seeds, toasted

Preheat the oven to 180°C (350°F).

Pour the stock into a clean saucepan and add the barley and ½ teaspoon salt. Bring the stock to the boil over a medium heat. Cook for 35 minutes until the stock has nearly evaporated and the barley is tender, stirring occasionally. Strain through a sieve and pour the barley onto a large flat tray. Drizzle with 2 tablespoons of the olive oil, season with salt and stir to coat, then spread out to cool completely.

Meanwhile, cut stems from the beetroot, leaving about 2 cm (1 in) from the top. Remove the leaves from the stems. Place the leaves in a bowl and set aside. Cut stems into 3 cm (1 in) pieces and set aside.

Place the beetroot and baby carrots on a roasting tray. Drizzle with 2 tablespoons olive oil, scatter with butter, season with salt and pepper, and toss to coat. Place in the oven for about 25 minutes until the vegetables are tender. Remove from oven and transfer to a bowl. Add 1 teaspoon of sherry vinegar and 1 teaspoon of the olive oil to the roasted vegetables and toss to coat. Season with salt and set aside.

Heirloom Root Vegetables with Barley and Goat's Cheese (cont.)

Place honey, champagne vinegar and 60 ml (2 fl oz/¼ cup) of water into a saucepan, and bring to the boil over medium heat. Remove from the heat, add the reserved beetroot stems and stir to combine.

To make the rocket pesto, blend the rocket, pine nuts and parmesan in the food processor until well combined. With the motor running, slowly add the remaining 60 ml (2 fl oz/¼ cup) of the olive oil. Season and set aside.

Pound the almonds, cumin seeds and ½ teaspoon salt in a mortar and pestle until ground.

To serve, smear the thick Greek yoghurt onto the serving plates. Drop spoonfuls of the rocket pesto onto the yoghurt. Sprinkle with a quarter of the barley and cumin and almond crumb.

Divide the beetroot and baby carrots among plates, then sprinkle with remaining barley and crumb mixture. Drain the beetroot stems well, then add to the plates with the leaves. Drizzle the servings with olive oil and season with salt.

This is amazing. Once you make this, it will be hard to go back to anything you have bought. Serve with little cornichons and freshly baked bread.

- -

Best-ever Chicken Liver Pâté with Homemade Bread

125 g (4 oz) butter
2 eschallots (shallots), finely chopped
6 rashers Dry-cured Bacon (see Basics), finely chopped
500 g (1 lb) chicken livers, cleaned and soaked for 1 hour in 500 ml/17½ fl oz water and 2 tablespoons salt)
3 tablespoons port

3 tablespoons cointreau
1 tablespoon brandy
½ cup thickened cream (35% fat)
50 g (1¾ oz) mushrooms, finely sliced
1 bay leaf
1 sprig thyme, stalk removed
salt and freshly ground black pepper, to taste
Easy Awesome Bread (see Basics), to serve

Heat the butter in a saucepan over a low heat. Sauté the onion and bacon slowly until very tender, but do not brown. Add the cleaned, drained livers and sauté for 3–4 minutes until just cooked.

Place the mixture into a blender.

Combine the port, cointreau, brandy, cream, mushrooms, bay leaf, thyme and salt and pepper in a pan, and bring to the boil. Simmer gently, uncovered, until the sauce has reduced by half. Remove the bay leaf. Pour the sauce into the blender with the liver and bacon mix. Blend everything until smooth.

Push the mixture through a coarse sieve and pour into smaller ramekins. Top with cling film loosely so that the cling film touches all of the pâté surface. Refrigerate until firm.

Serve with bread and cornichons—wine optional, but recommended.

When I visit my sister Rachel we go kayaking over to a little beach area and pick fresh mussels off the rocks and take them home. Collecting fresh mussels is made only better by grabbing a few handfuls of samphire on the beach to add to the pot. I love this way of eating!

Mussels My Way

1 eschalot (shallot), peeled, sliced
2 cloves garlic, finely chopped
1 tablespoon olive oil
½–1 cm long red fresh chilli, deseeded and chopped
1 kg/36 oz mussels

few handfuls of samphire, if you can find it
1 cup white wine
2 handfuls flat-leafed parsley, chopped
2 tablespoons butter, to serve
1 loaf Easy Awesome Bread (see Basics), to serve

Heat a wok or a wide pan over medium-low heat. Sauté the eschalot and garlic in the olive oil. Add the chilli and sauté for a minute or two.

Add the mussels and samphire. Turn the heat up and add the white wine. Put a lid on and shake the pan while still on the heat. As soon as the mussels open, remove the pan from the heat—this should take only a few minutes. Take out all mussels that haven't opened and discard.

Toss in the parsley and butter and serve with freshly baked bread.

Chestnuts are in season in winter and are the perfect food to forage for! I think chestnuts are the most commonly foraged ingredient as they are easy to identify and grow all around the world. What to do with them once you've gathered some up? Roast and make soup!

Roast Chestnut and Puy Lentil Soup

serves 4–6

200 g (6½ oz) chestnuts (shell on)
1 large red onion, finely diced
4 cloves garlic, peeled and finely chopped
1 carrot, finely sliced
1 stick celery, finely sliced
½ leek, finely diced
3 sage leaves
1 sprig thyme
1 sprig rosemary

80 g (2½ oz) Dry-cured Bacon (see Basics)
6 (about 200 g/7 oz) plum/cherry tomatoes, chopped
500 g (17½ oz) puy lentils
2 litres (70 fl oz) water or chicken stock
black pepper (5 twists of the mill)
handful parsley leaves, chopped, to serve

Preheat the oven to 200°C (400°F).

Cut a cross into the top of each chestnut with a small knife then place them on a baking tray and roast for about 15 minutes, until the husks are coming away from the chestnuts.

Heat a large heavy-based saucepan and lightly sauté the onion, garlic, carrot, celery, leek, sage, thyme, rosemary and bacon.

Peel the chestnuts then finely chop two-thirds of them and slice the remaining third to use for decoration and set aside. Add the chopped chestnuts to the pan of vegetables.

In a large pan, add the chopped tomatoes, puy lentils and water or stock and bring to a boil. Simmer and cook for about an hour until the lentils are soft. If you like the soup thicker, take out a third and blend until smooth and return to the chunky soup.

Season to taste, garnish with sliced chestnuts and parsley.

A haunch of venison is the equivalent cut of meat as the rump on a cow. It is beautifully tender and my preferred cut over the more expensive fillet.

- -

Roast Haunch of Venison with Smoked Mash, Spinach and Nutmeg

800 g (28 oz) venison haunch or fillet, cut into
    4 x 200 g (7 oz) pieces
salt and pepper, to season
2 tablespoons vegetable oil
50 g (1¾ oz) pitted cherries
100 ml (3½ oz) My Rich and Luxurious Jus
   (see Basics)
400 g (14 oz) spinach

knob of butter
½ nutmeg, grated
salt and pepper, to taste

SMOKED MASH
1 kg (36 oz) Nicola potatoes
salt, to season
250 g (9 oz) Smoked Butter (see Basics), diced

Preheat the oven to 180°C (350°F).

Make your mash. Peel and cut the potatoes into quarters. Place in a suitably large pot, cover with water and bring to a simmer with a large pinch of salt. I like to boil my potatoes for mash until they are just about falling apart which takes about 30 minutes.

Meanwhile, season the venison haunch fillets with salt and pepper. Heat a little vegetable oil in a large ovenproof saucepan or baking dish over a high heat. Place the venison fillets carefully in the hot pan and sauté. Once caramelised nicely on two sides, flip them onto the third side (the fourth side doesn't get cooked here), and then place in the oven for 4 minutes.

Remove from oven and allow the meat to rest on a cooling rack.

Drain the spuds and leave to steam dry in the colander for a few minutes then pass through a mouli or fine sieve. Mix in the smoked butter and season to taste. Set aside.

Add the cherries to the same pan you cooked the venison in (no need to wash the pan: we want those pan juices). Sauté for 1 minute before deglazing the pan with your pre-prepared jus. Set aside.

Finally, wilt down your spinach with a knob of butter and the nutmeg in the same pan, and season to taste. Plate up!

I am currently obsessed with nasturtium capers. My nasturtiums grow pretty wild and they drop their seedpods everywhere! You can pickle them and they take on the same characteristics as regular capers, which is pretty neat! This recipe requires a bit of forward planning and you need to begin a few days in advance (or a month if you are pickling nasturtium pods). If you are not using nasturtium capers, then regular store-bought capers will do the trick.

Crispy-skinned Fish with Lemon-smashed Potatoes, Nasturtiums and Pickled Lemon

serves 4

800 g (28 oz) Dutch cream potatoes, peeled and halved
2 tablespoons Easy Lemon Dressing (see Basics)
4 x 150 g (5 oz) fillets sea bream
olive oil, for frying
20 nasturtium leaves (approx.)

NASTURTIUM CAPERS
3 teaspoons salt
300 ml (10½ fl oz) water

100 g (3½ oz) nasturtium seed pods (try to get small ones)
200 ml (7 fl oz) white wine vinegar

PICKLED LEMONS
300 g (10½ oz) water
150 g (5 oz) caster (superfine) sugar
250 g (9 oz) white wine vinegar
4 lemons, thinly sliced

To make the nasturtium capers, make a light brine by dissolving the salt in the water. Soak the nasturtium pods for 24 hours. Drain the pods and put them into a sterilised jar. Cover with white wine vinegar. Store the jar in a cool dark place for a month before using.

Pickle the lemons by bringing the water, sugar and vinegar to the boil. Once cool, add the sliced lemons. Leave for at least two days to marinate in the fridge before using.

Place the potatoes in a large pot and cover with water. Bring to the boil and simmer for 20 minutes until tender. Drain. Toss the Easy Lemon Dressing through the potatoes and set aside.

Place the bream fillets in a cool non-stick frying pan over a low to medium heat with a dash of olive oil. Use a fish slice to put some pressure on the fillets just as they start to fry to prevent their skin from puckering up.

Cook on low heat until the skin is crispy and, once crispy, flip the fish over for 20 seconds and remove from pan.

Add 1 cup of vegetable oil to a small fry pan and heat to 180°C (350°F). Have a mesh spoon handy. Put the nasturtium capers, or regular capers (pictured) into the hot oil, they will open like a flower and sizzle— remove immediately.

Serve fish with pickled lemon, deep-fried capers, fresh nasturtium leaves and lemon potatoes.

These sliders are cute, colourful and so moreish! They are perfect to serve to a crowd as you will have plenty of pulled pork to go around.

Pulled Pork Sliders with Chipotle Mayonnaise

serves 8

50 g (1½ oz) sea salt
50 g (1½ oz) dark brown sugar
30 g (1½ oz) smoked paprika
10 g (⅓ oz) ground cumin
1.5 kg (53 oz) free-range pork shoulder, on the bone, neck end
1 stick celery halved
1 carrot, halved
2 tomatoes halved
½ onion

8 peppercorns
2 bay leaves
small bunch thyme
1 quantity Slider Milk Buns with Wild Fennel Seeds (see Basics)

CHIPOTLE MAYONNAISE
½ x 340 g (12 oz) can chipotle chillies in adobo sauce (I prefer La Costena brand)
½ cup Homemade Mayonnaise (see Basics)

Preheat the oven to 220°C (420°F).

Mix salt, sugar, paprika and cumin together. Rub half of the spice mixture into the pork all over the outside. Place in an ovenproof dish and add celery, carrot, tomatoes, onion, peppercorns, bay leaves and thyme, and cover with 1.5 litres (52fl oz) of water.

Cook in the oven for at least 3½ hours or until the pork pulls away. Alternatively, place into a pressure cooker and cover with water. Cook at pressure for 1½–2 hours. Remove from heat.

Leave to cool for 30 minutes. Remove the pork from the stock and pull the meat off the bone. Heat stock and reduce the liquid by one-third. Mix back into the pulled pork meat. Add the remaining seasonings to taste.

To make the mayonnaise, take 2 spoonfuls of the chillies from the can, then keep the rest in the fridge in a sealed container for another use (sticky beef ribs for example see page 198).

Blend the chillies to a fine paste (either in a mortar and pestle or a hand blender) and mix the paste with the mayonnaise. This will add a great kick to your sliders.

Assemble the milk buns with the pulled pork, Pink Coleslaw with Horseradish (see recipe page 102) and chipotle mayonaise.

Horseradish is a wonderful plant to grow in the garden. You can plant it in the corner of your veggie patch and it grows happily without much attention. It does need to be in the ground, or a deep pot as it has a large tap root. Horseradish is a companion plant for potatoes as it helps to prevent potato blight. Fresh horseradish is worlds apart from the pre-prepared stuff you buy in the jar.

- -

Pink Coleslaw with Wild Horseradish

1 red onion, peeled, halved and thinly sliced
1 fennel bulb, halved and thinly sliced
½ red cabbage, sliced finely
1 fresh beetroot, grated
1 baby turnip, very finely sliced
2 cm (1 in) fresh horseradish, grated
½ cup Homemade Mayonnaise (see Basics)
salt, to taste

Combine all of the vegetables in a bowl. Mix the horseradish and mayonnaise together and stir through the salad to create a lovely pink coleslaw.

Fabulous with sticky beef ribs or pork, pulled pork especially.

Tea Time

Sweets and Treats

Who am I kidding? I love an excuse to eat cake!

That is why I love it when people drop by. There is nothing better than friends

or family popping around for a cup of tea. The recipes in this section are brought

together because they are all lovely recipes to share at tea time.

I think it is baking that really gets kids into cooking and I was no exception. I

have been baking my Grannie's yo yos in this chapter for many years and now

these are firm favourites of my nieces and nephews. Some things never change.

The recipes in this section include fail-safe cake recipes that my family and

friends have enjoyed, although now many have my influence (such as the honey

thyme cake—which is now Dan's favourite).

I have tried to include a broad selection of sweet treats for you to try and they're

my top hitters! All killer, no filler here.

Jo is one of my best friends, and she often requests this for her birthday and I love to make it for her! I have since added the thyme, which is stunning with honey and almonds!

Honey Thyme Cake

serves 10

90 g (3 oz) butter, melted
4 eggs
185 g (6 oz) caster (superfine) sugar
zest of 2 lemons
60 ml (2 fl oz) cream
90 g (3 oz) self-raising (self-rising) flour,
 sifted

TOPPING
2 cups flaked almonds
90 g (3 oz) butter
90 g (3 oz) caster (superfine) sugar
60 ml (2 fl oz) cream
2 tablespoons honey
2 heaped teaspoons fresh thyme leaves

Preheat the oven to 180°C (350°F). Grease and line a deep 20 cm (8 in) round pan.

Beat the eggs and sugar in a large bowl until thick and pale. Using a spatula, fold in the lemon zest, butter and cream in batches. Fold in the flour. Pour into the prepared tin and bake for 40 minutes until firm in the centre.

When the cake is nearly ready, make the almond topping by combining all the ingredients in a saucepan. Stir over a medium heat and bring to the boil. Turn off the heat and pour the hot mixture over the top of the cake.

Put the cake back in the oven for 10 minutes or until the topping turns golden. Remove from the oven and allow the cake to cool in the tin.

Once cool, remove the cake from the tin and place on a serving plate. This is fabulous with whipped cream.

These are incredibly nostalgic for me—great to have with a cup of tea and made with freshly picked passionfruit from my backyard. Grannie used to freeze passionfruit pulp and make ice blocks for us and that taste will forever remind me of her.

Grannie's Yo Yos

190 g (6½ oz) butter
60 g (2 oz) icing (confectioners') sugar
190 g (6½ oz) plain (all-purpose) flour
60 g (2 oz) custard powder

PASSIONFRUIT FILLING
2 cups icing (confectioners') sugar, sifted
pulp from 1–2 passionfruits (depending on
   their size)

Preheat the oven to 160°C (320°F) and line a baking sheet (cookie sheet) with baking paper.

In a large bowl, cream the butter and sugar together. Add the flour and custard powder in batches and mix to make a dough.

Roll the dough into small balls and place on the baking paper at even intervals. Flatten with a fork—dip the fork into flour every few presses to prevent the fork from sticking to the dough.

Bake for 17–20 minutes or until lightly coloured. Remove from the oven and set aside on a wire rack to cool.

Mix together the icing sugar and passionfruit pulp, to a very stiff consistency. Once the biscuits are cool, wedge two biscuits together with the passionfruit icing in the middle.

I love this family favourite because it is so easy and everyone raves about it—from my young nephew Max to my great Auntie Nellie. It's robust too! With a few layers of cling film, this cake will travel well and survive a bike trip or a picnic. This cake is also gluten free.

Orange Chocolate Cake

2 oranges
6 eggs
250 g (9 oz) caster (superfine) sugar
250 g (9 oz) almond meal
1 teaspoon baking powder

½ teaspoon bicarbonate of soda (baking soda)
50 g (1¾ oz) best quality cocoa powder
cocoa, to dust, or candied orange peel, to serve

Preheat the oven to 180°C (350°F) and prepare a 20 cm (8 in) round lined tin.

Put the oranges whole in a pressure cooker and cover entirely with water. Put the lid on and bring up to pressure. Once at pressure, cook the oranges for about 12 minutes. Alternatively, simmer on the stove top for 2 hours. Cool slightly.

Cut the oranges in half (across the middle of the fruit) and take out as many seeds as you can. Add the oranges and the rest of the ingredients to a food processor and pulse until combined. Don't over-mix—it's good to still see chunks of orange peel.

Pour the batter into the tin. Bake for 1 hour. Check after 45 minutes to stop it getting too brown on the top. If it is, cover the top with foil and keep baking.

Once cooked, remove the cake from the oven and cool in the tin.

Remove from tin and dust with cocoa or candied orange peel. Serve with double cream if you want, but it tastes delicious just by itself.

Doughnuts. Caramel. Needs no introduction! Although please do use scales to measure your ingredients, especially when using yeast, as a slight imbalance of ingredients will kill your yeast.

Doughnuts with Caramel Sauce

60 g (2 oz) unsalted butter
250 ml (9 oz) full-fat milk
7 g (one sachet) dry yeast
500 g (1 1/2 oz) strong bread flour, sifted
290 g (10 oz) caster (superfine) sugar
10 g (1/3 oz) salt
2 large eggs, lightly beaten
1 teaspoon cinnamon, mixed through
vegetable oil, for frying

1 egg, whisked for wash

CARAMEL SAUCE
200 g (7 oz) caster (superfine) sugar
50 ml (1 3/4 fl oz) water
150 ml (5 fl oz) thickened cream
pinch of sea salt
1 tablespoon butter

To make the doughnuts, add the butter to the milk and warm until it melts (stovetop or microwave is fine). Make sure it doesn't go over 60°C (140°F) so the heat doesn't kill the yeast.

In an electric mixer, stir together the yeast, flour, 2 tablespoons sugar and salt. Using the dough attachment, add the melted butter mixture and pour in the beaten eggs. Mix for 5 minutes and finish the dough off by hand, kneading for about 5 minutes—this is a sticky dough!

Shape into 30 g (1 oz) balls of dough. Place on a lined baking tray and leave to prove in a warm place under a tea towel for 30–40 minutes until the balls have doubled in size to about the size of a small peach.

In a small bowl, mix the rest of the caster sugar together with the cinnamon and set next to the deep fryer.

Heat oil to 180°C (350°F) in the deep-fryer. Place the doughnuts carefully into the hot oil and fry them for 1–2 minutes until they are golden all over. Keep them moving with a slotted spoon. Remove from oil and drain on kitchen paper before tossing them immediately into the cinnamon and sugar mixture.

Doughnuts with Caramel Sauce (cont.)

To make the caramel sauce, combine the sugar and water in a heavy-based saucepan and leave to soak together for a few minutes. This helps prevent crystallisation. Turn the heat to high and bring to the boil without stirring. After 5 minutes, or when little clouds of dark syrup start to form, shake the pan a little. When the entire mixture turns to a dark caramel colour and you can smell a slightly bitter aroma, quickly remove the pan from the heal.

Immediately, stir in the cream. Beware: the mixture will bubble and spit profusely at this point! Then add a pinch of sea salt and butter. Gently mix with a whisk. Pour the caramel into a small dish.

You are ready to dip your doughnuts in! Pick them up with a fork and coat with the caramel. Or just pour all the sauce over a pile of doughnuts. This sauce is also great on ice cream.

These are a cheeky way to enjoy fresh raspberries from the garden. I originally used Annie Smithers' recipe for Pot au Crème. The raspberries and cream really highlight the smooth chocolate.

Chocolate and Raspberry Pots

375 ml (13 fl oz) thickened cream (35% fat)
250 ml (9 fl oz) full-fat milk
1 vanilla pod, seeds removed
½ cup caster (superfine) sugar
250 g (14 oz) dark chocolate, chopped

6 egg yolks
300 ml (10½ oz) thickened cream
1 cup fresh raspberries

Preheat the oven to 160°C (320°F). Line a roasting tray with a tea towel. This will prevent the ramekins from sliding around stops the heat conducting fiercely through the bottom of the pots when they are cooking.

In a small saucepan, bring the cream, milk, vanilla seeds and pod, and sugar to the boil, stirring gently with a spatula.

Remove from heat and add the chocolate. Mix until it is dissolved and smooth.

Set aside to cool a little.

In a bowl, lightly beat the egg yolks. Pour them onto the cool chocolate mixture, whisking gently. Strain the mixture and pour into 6–8 ovenproof ramekins.

Place a folded tea towel in the bottom of a deep roasting tray. Place the ramekins on the tea towel and then pour boiling water into the roasting tray, so that the water goes up halfway up the sides of the ramekins. Cover the entire baking tray with foil.

Bake for 45 minutes or until set. Remove from the oven and transfer the ramekins to the refrigerator to cool.

Whisk the cream until stiff. Place in a piping bag and pipe it onto the chocolate pot ramekins. Dot the raspberries around the outside of the cream.

Serve cold.

These are just lovely to eat on a summer afternoon! They are a great picnic addition, or make a delightful treat for catching up with friends. Sweet, tart and with flaky pastry to boot— what's not to love?

Rhubarb Frangipane Tarts

makes 10

1 quantity Rough Puff Pastry (see Basics)

FRANGIPANE
100 g (3½ oz) almond meal
100 g (3½ oz) unsalted butter, softened
100 g (3½ oz) caster (superfine) sugar
1 egg
½ vanilla pod, seeds removed
zest of ½ orange

RHUBARB FILLING
5 stalks rhubarb
juice and zest of 1 orange
juice and zest of 1 lemon
60 g (2 oz) caster (superfine) sugar

vanilla ice cream or clotted cream, to serve

Firstly, make the pastry following the instructions.

Mix all the frangipane ingredients together in a bowl and set aside.

Preheat the oven to 175°C (350°F) and line a baking tin with baking paper.

Cut the rhubarb into 8 cm (4 in) lengths. Place the lengths onto the baking paper. Sprinkle with juice, zest and sugar. Cover with tin foil. Bake for 12–15 minutes (depending on the thickness of your rhubarb).

Roll out the pastry and cut into rectangles about 10 x 5 cm (4 x 2 in).

Smear about 4 teaspoons of frangipane onto each piece of the pastry. Place some rhubarb batons on top of each square of pastry and frangipane. Place the squares on a baking tray lined with baking paper. Bake at 190°C (375°F) for 10–15 minutes.

Remove from the oven and cool on a wire rack. Serve with vanilla ice cream or clotted cream.

Ah, bananas! There's always one that escapes your attention; no sooner have you turned your back on it, it is black and soft. But not to worry: use those over-ripened bananas in this delicious cake—the spice additions make a welcome treat to a traditional recipe. Yum!

Spicy Banana Cake

serves 10

125 g (4 oz) unsalted butter, at room
   temperature
125 g (4 oz) caster (superfine) sugar
2 eggs
1 vanilla pod, seeds removed
4 really ripe bananas, peeled and mashed
1 teaspoon bicarbonate of soda (baking soda)
½ cup full-fat milk
2 tablespoons cognac
300 g (10½ oz) self-raising (self-rising) flour,
   sifted

1 teaspoon ground cinnamon
½ teaspoon ground cardamom
½ teaspoon allspice
½ teaspoon ground ginger

TOPPING
125 g (4 oz) unsalted butter, at room
   temperature
¾ cup icing (confectioners') sugar, sifted
1 tablespoon lemon juice
½ cup coconut flakes, toasted

Preheat the oven to 180°C (350°F). Grease and line a 20 cm (8 in) round cake tin.

Cream the butter and sugar in a mixing bowl until it is light and fluffy. Add the eggs one at a time followed by the vanilla seeds and the bananas. Beat everything until combined.

In a small bowl, dissolve the bicarbonate of soda into the milk and cognac. Sift the flour and spices together in a separate bowl.

Using a spatula, fold the milk mixture and the flour in alternating batches into the banana mixture until all ingredients are combined and the mixture is smooth.

Pour the mixture into a prepared tin and bake for 1 hour or until a skewer comes out clean. Leave to cool in tin for 10 minutes and turn out onto wire rack.

Make the topping by beating the butter, icing sugar and lemon juice together until light and fluffy. Spread over the cooled cake and top with coconut flakes. If your icing sugar has hard lumps in it, blitz it in the food processor before you sift it.

This is a sophisticated take on the caramel slice. This is a fabulous transportable slice that you will love. You will never look at caramel slices in the same way again. The slightly salted olive oil shortbread adds a grown-up element, which makes the caramel pop. I've included a trick for tempering chocolate, too.

Caramel and Olive Oil Shortbread

115 g (4 oz) unsalted butter
100 g (3½ oz) caster (superfine) sugar
125 g (4½ oz) plain (all-purpose) flour, sifted
50 g (1¾ oz) almond meal
½ teaspoon salt
½ vanilla pod, seeds removed
25 g (¾ oz) olive oil
1 egg yolk
200 g (7 oz) dark eating chocolate (I use
    Lindt 70% cocoa), for topping

CARAMEL
1 x 440 g (15 oz) evaporated milk
250 g (9 oz) unsalted butter
125 g (4 oz) demerara sugar

In a large bowl, cream the butter and sugar together. Stir in the dry ingredients. Mix in the vanilla seeds, olive oil and egg yolk.

Form the dough into a ball and refrigerate for 20 minutes.

Preheat the oven to 160°C (320°F).

Roll out the dough between two sheets of baking paper, to ½ cm (¼ in) thick. Transfer the dough into a large loaf tin, leaving about 5 cm (2 in) of paper above the top of the tin on two sides so you can lift out the finished shortbread for cutting. Trim the sides of the dough so it fits neatly on the bottom. Remove the top layer of baking paper.

Prick the dough numerous times with a fork and then bake for 30 minutes (you don't blind bake this—you are making a biscuit).

Caramel and Olive Oil Shortbread (cont.)

- -

Remove the tin from the oven and allow to cool slightly. Keep the shortbread in the tin.

Combine the evaporated milk, butter and sugar in a saucepan and bring to the boil. Turn the heat down and let the mixture simmer for about 10 to 15 minutes. Stir constantly, as it thickens. Scrape down the sides and keep on stirring. Make sure all the surface area of the saucepan has been stirred in. After 25 minutes the caramel will be thick and glossy and will set on the spoon. Pour it over the shortbread and smooth with a palette knife. There should be about 2 cm (1 in) of caramel on top of the shortbread.

Melt the block of dark chocolate in a double boiler until just melted. If it is already tempered (i.e. it snaps when you eat it) don't go over 31°C (88°F) when you melt it and it will stay tempered—your friends will be impressed that you tempered chocolate! Pour the melted chocolate over the caramel, shaking the tin so all the caramel is covered. Leave in the refrigerator for about 10–15 minutes to cool and set.

Pull the shortbread out of the tin using the baking paper at the sides and lift it onto a chopping board. Trim the edges of the slice and cut it into 2 cm (1 in) squares. Make sure you wipe the knife after each slice. Arrange on a lovely plate!

This is so delicious! I can't believe that a vegetable tastes so good as an ice cream, but this does. It is adventurous, a little bit different, and I urge you to try it out.

- -

Jerusalem Artichoke Ice Cream and Poached Pears

4 egg yolks
125 g (4 oz) caster (superfine) sugar plus
   1 tablespoon
250 g (9 oz) full-fat milk
½ vanilla pod, seeds removed
250 g (9 oz) thickened cream (35% fat)
300 g (10½ oz) Jerusalem artichokes, peeled
   and thinly sliced
2 tablespoons butter
pinch of salt

POACHED PEARS
250 ml (9 fl oz) white wine
250 ml (9 fl oz) water
250 g (9 oz) white sugar
1 cinnamon stick
1 star anise
1 vanilla pod, halved
4 pears, peeled, cored and halved

toasted coconut, to serve

Whisk the egg yolks and sugar until thick, creamy and ribbony. Bring the milk, tablespoon of sugar and vanilla seeds and pod to boil in a medium-sized saucepan. Remove the vanilla pod and reserve for use in the poached pears. Whisk the hot milk into the egg yolk mixture and then return the mixture to the saucepan. Using a spatula, mix the custard over a medium heat and cook until thickened (between 80–85°C/175–185°F). Once thickened, stir in the cream. Remove from the heat and allow to cool.

In a saucepan, sauté the Jerusalem artichokes in the butter for a few minutes. Once heated through, but not yet browning, add enough water to just cover. Cook gently until soft, adding more water as needed to keep them covered. Don't let this simmer dry or add too much water.

Once cooked, transfer the artichokes to a food processor, add a pinch of salt, and blend until smooth. Leave to cool in the processor. Add the ice cream mixture to the artichoke mixture and blend well.

Strain the mixture through a sieve and transfer to an ice cream machine and churn until set. Transfer to a freezer to fully set, for at least 2 hours.

Jerusalem Artichoke Ice Cream and Poached Pears (cont.)

- -

To poach the pears, combine white wine, water, sugar and spices in a pan and bring to the boil. Reduce to a gentle simmer and add the pears. Make a cartouche (see below) and place it on top of the pears while they are cooking. On top of the cartouche place a small side plate. This will submerge the pears and prevent any uncooked spots.

To assemble, place a pear in a bowl and drizzle over some poaching liquid. Serve with a ball of the delicious Jerusalem artichoke ice cream and sprinkle over some toasted coconut.

How to make a cartouche: Get your craft on. Cut a piece of baking paper larger than your saucepan. Fold the paper in half, then fold in half again. You should then have a small rectangular shape. Holding one corner, fold it again into a triangle, then fold it in half again so the paper looks like a flat cone. Take the tip of your cone and place it in the centre of your pan, laying the rest of the cone out to one edge of the pan. Make a little tear at the large end of your cone where it meets the edge of your pan. Tear across, making a triangle. Undo your baking paper and hooray-you have a circle of baking paper that fits inside your pan. You have just made a cartouche.

This is an incredible recipe—super easy, no tricky custard making and no taking the mixture to a certain temperature. It's a kind of melt, cool and churn type of thing! The honeycomb is an added treat.

Yoghurt Sorbet and Honeycomb

serves 4–6

YOGHURT SORBET
100 g (3½ oz) caster (superfine) sugar
100 g (3½ oz) liquid glucose
200 g (7 oz) water
500 g (17½ oz) Greek yoghurt

HONEYCOMB
100 g (3½ oz) caster (superfine) sugar
95 g (3½ oz) glucose syrup
1 tablespoon honey
2 teaspoons bicarbonate of soda (baking soda)
1 teaspoon water

Line a small loaf tin with baking paper.

To make the honeycomb, bring the sugar and glucose to a boil until it reaches a temperature of 140°C (285°F). Remove from the heat and add the honey. Mix. Then add the bicarbonate of soda and the water, stirring quickly to combine as it froths up. Pour quickly into a loaf tin. Leave to cool and set. Wow—honeycomb!

To make the sorbet, combine the sugar, liquid glucose and water and stir over a medium heat to dissolve (no need to boil). Remove from heat and cool. Add the yoghurt and mix well. Place into the ice cream machine and churn until set. Place in the freezer to firm up properly—about 2 hours.

Serve the yoghurt sorbet with some crumbled honeycomb. Or try serving it with fresh fruit, berries, salted caramel or you could even sprinkle chrysanthemum petals over the top.

A Homegrown Table

These gingernuts are fabulous by themselves and just a little bit more fabulous with poached quince and mascarpone.

Poached Quinces with Mascarpone and Gingernuts

GINGERNUT BISCUITS
makes at least 24 (so you'll have a few extra for a cup of tea or two)

125 g (4 oz) unsalted butter, at room temperature
1 cup caster (superfine) sugar
¼ cup treacle
1 egg
300 g (10½ oz) plain (all-purpose) flour
1½ teaspoons bicarbonate of soda (baking soda)
2 teaspoons cinnamon
2 teaspoons ground ginger

1 teaspoon allspice
raw (granulated) sugar, for rolling

POACHED QUINCES
250 ml (9 fl oz) rosé wine
250 ml (9 fl oz) water
250 g (9 oz) caster (superfine) sugar
1 cinnamon stick
2 star anise
1 bay leaf
4 quinces, peeled, cored and halved

1 cup mascarpone cheese, to serve

Preheat the oven to 180°C (350°F). Line a baking tray (cookie sheet) with baking paper.

To make the biscuits, cream the butter and sugar until light and fluffy. Beat in the treacle and egg. Sift in the rest of the ingredients, except the sugar for rolling, and mix everything until combined.

Pour the raw sugar onto a small plate. Portion out teaspoon-sized balls of mixture and roll into balls. Roll the balls into the raw sugar and place on the lined baking tray. Press down on the balls with a fork.

Bake for 10 minutes and then cool on a rack.

Poached Quinces with Mascarpone and Gingernuts (cont.)

- -

To make the poached quinces, combine the rosé, water, sugar and spices, and bring to the boil. Add the quince halves and simmer on a medium heat until soft. If quinces are not submerged, add additional water and then cover with a cartouche (see How to make a cartouche page 131). Drain and reserve the poaching liquid.

Crush 4 gingernut biscuits into large crumbs and fold into the mascarpone cheese.

To serve, place one half of a quince in a serving bowl and pour over some poaching liquid. Top with the gingernut mascarpone and some crumbled gingernut biscuits over the top.

Delish!

Note: If you want the beautiful red colour of quinces to come through when you poach them, poach quinces slowly, in an ovenproof dish with a lid on, in the oven at 140°C (285°F), with the above ingredients, for 2-3 hours. You should add the cores from the fruit into the liquid as the additional pectin in the cores assist in the ruby colour formation.

I made this cake for Dan for his birthday using freshly picked raspberries from my garden. He was so chuffed, he said that I should audition to go on the show—so this cake is pretty special. I also think the icing is great, as it is completely artificial colour free, so it's good for everyone.

- -

Raspberry Cream Sponge

SPONGE
4 eggs
170 g (6 oz) caster (superfine) sugar
1 vanilla pod, seeds removed
130 g (4½ oz) corn flour (corn starch)
1 teaspoon cream of tartar
½ teaspoon bicarbonate of soda (baking soda)
¾ cup Berry Jam (see Basics), to serve

1½ cups thickened cream, whipped, to serve

RASPBERRY TOPPING
1 cup fresh raspberries
320 g (11 oz) icing (confectioners') sugar
1 tablespoon unsalted butter, softened
2 teaspoons hot water

Preheat the oven to 180°C (350°F).

Cream the eggs and sugar for 10 minutes until thick and creamy. Add the vanilla seeds.

Sift together the rest of the dry ingredients and fold into the egg mixture. Spread into a 22 cm (8½ in) round cake pan (buttered and floured) and bake for 25 minutes, or until a skewer comes out clean. Leave to cool for 5 minutes before removing from the tin and leaving on a wire rack.

To make the topping, push the raspberries through a sieve to remove all of the seeds. Sift the icing sugar into the raspberry purée. Stir in the butter, enough to make a paste. Place the bowl over hot water and stir until the mixture is spreadable, adding a teaspoon or two of hot water as needed.

When the cake is cool, slice it gently in half, using a bread knife. Spread the bottom half generously with Berry Jam and softly whipped cream, then place the top half back on. Spread the raspberry icing on top.

Cut into wedges and enjoy!

This is also delicious with passionfruit icing and strawberry jam in the centre.

My mum makes this and I just love it. This is a very easy recipe and really showcases the rhubarb.

- -

Rhubarb Cake

serves 10

50 g (1¾ oz) unsalted butter, melted
2 cups raw (granulated) sugar
2 eggs
½ vanilla pod, seeds removed (or 1 teaspoon
   vanilla extract)
2 cups plain (all-purpose) flour
1 teaspoon bicarbonate of soda (baking soda)

2 teaspoons cinnamon
500 g (17½ oz) trimmed rhubarb, cut into
   1 cm pieces
250 g (9 oz) sour cream
zest and juice of 1 orange
¼ cup brown sugar
double cream, to serve

Preheat the oven to 180°C (350°F). Grease a 22 cm (8½ in) round spring-form tin and line with baking paper.

In a large bowl, beat the butter, sugar, eggs and vanilla seeds until thick and creamy.

Sift together the flour, bicarbonate of soda and 1 teaspoon cinnamon and mix into the egg mixture. Mix until combined. Stir in the rhubarb, sour cream and 2 teaspoons orange zest.

Pour into the prepared cake tin and smooth out. Combine the brown sugar and remaining cinnamon and sprinkle over the top.

Bake for 1 hour and 20 minutes, or until a skewer comes out clean. Immediately after you take the cake out of the oven, drizzle the fresh orange juice over the top.

Serve warm or cold with double cream—this cake is delicious.

Note: To preserve the glut of summer rhubarb, you can simply freeze rhubarb in whole fresh stalks in freezer bags. This cake also works wonderfully with defrosted rhubarb.

Tea Time

One of my first memories of a now very dear friend of mine, Lil, is this whole citrus cake. This cake is delicious and Lil has given the recipe to me to share here. This is a dense cake, which gives a fabulous citrus hit.

Whole Citrus Cake

serves 10

1 orange
1 lemon
125 g (4 oz) unsalted butter
¾ cup caster (superfine) sugar
2 eggs
1½ cups self-raising (self-rising) flour
½ cup Homemade Buttermilk (see Basics)
double cream, to serve

SYRUP
1 cup caster (superfine) sugar
½ cup orange juice
½ cup lemon juice

Preheat the oven to 180°C (350°F). Grease and line a 22 cm (8½ in) springform cake tin.

Boil the whole fruit until soft (about 2 hours on the stove or 15 minutes in a pressure cooker). Cut in half to flick out the seeds, then blend in a food processor.

Cream the butter and the sugar until pale and thick. Beat in the eggs and fold in the flour and buttermilk. Fold in the puréed citrus fruit.

Bake for 45 minutes, or until a skewer inserted into the middle of the cake comes out clean. Leave the cake to cool in the tin.

To make the syrup, boil the fruit juices and sugar together without stirring and pour over the hot cake. I like to prick the top of the cake several times with a skewer to assist with the syrup absorption.

Serve warm with double cream.

A Homegrown Table

This is decadent and versatile as you can serve this with any in-season fruits—I usually alternate between poached quinces or raspberries. This is also gluten free.

Chocolate Almond Torte

serves 10

250 g (9 oz) 70% cocoa eating chocolate
2 tablespoons espresso coffee
2 tablespoons brandy
180 g (6 oz) almond meal
180 g (6 oz) unsalted butter
180 g (6 oz) caster (superfine) sugar
6 eggs, separated
double cream, to serve
fresh or poached fruits (I used sliced Poached
    Quinces in the photo (see recipe page 135),
    to serve

Preheat the oven to 170°C (340°F). Grease a slab tin with a removable base.

In a small saucepan, melt the chocolate, coffee and brandy together over a low heat. Add the butter and stir until the butter is melted. Add in the almond meal and sugar, stirring to combine.

Remove from the heat and allow to cool a little. Beat in the yolks, one at a time.

Whisk the egg whites until soft peaks form. Fold the egg whites into the chocolate mixture one-third at a time.

Pour into a buttered slab tin and bake for 40–45 minutes. If you have any leftover mixture, pour it into buttered muffin tins and bake for 20 minutes.

Serve with double cream and fresh or poached fruits, depending on the season.

I have a lime tree that is over 10 years old, growing out of a half—wine barrel. It happily gives me my yearly supply of limes. I love having limes fresh waiting for me whenever I might need them, either for a refreshing drink in the evening, or for a simple but elegant dessert such as this posset. The butter fingers are delicious dipped into the posset, or simply by themselves.

Set Lime Posset and Butter Fingers

makes 6 delicate serves

A Homegrown Table

LIME POSSET
200 g (7 oz) caster (superfine) sugar
600 ml (21 fl oz) thickened cream (35% fat)
zest and juice of 3 limes

BUTTER FINGERS
(makes about 40)
125 g (4 oz) unsalted butter, softened
125 g (4 oz) icing (confectioners') sugar
1 teaspoon vanilla extract
2 small egg whites, lightly whisked
175 g (6 oz) plain (all-purpose) flour
flaked salt, to serve

Preheat the oven to 170°C (340°F). Line a baking tray with paper.

To make the butter fingers, cream butter and icing sugar together until light and fluffy. Add vanilla and egg whites, and mix in well. Fold in the flour using a large metal spoon.

Put the mixture into a piping bag fitted with a 5 mm (¼ in) nozzle. Pipe straight lines of batter onto a lined baking sheet (cookie tray), leaving the space as they do spread a little.

Bake for 8–10 minutes. The edges should be just beginning to turn golden. Cool slightly and then remove from the baking tray, to a wire rack to cool completely.

To make the lime posset, mix sugar and cream in a pan and bring slowly to the boil—boil for 3 minutes. Take off the heat and add the zest and juice, mixing well. Pour into serving glasses, tea cups, ramekins, espresso cups—whatever you intend to serve it in.

Place in the refrigerator to set; this should take about 4–6 hours.

Gingerbread with Rhubarb and Honey Ice Cream

HONEY ICE CREAM
250 ml (9 fl oz) full-fat milk
vanilla pod, seeds removed
5 egg yolks
50 g (1¾ oz) caster (superfine) sugar
50 g (1¾ oz) best-quality honey
250 ml (9 fl oz) thickened cream (35% fat)

RHUBARB
4 stalks of rhubarb, cut into 5 cm (2 in) pieces
zest and juice of ½ lemon
zest and juice of ½ orange
¼ cup caster (superfine) sugar

GINGERBREAD
60 g (2 oz) unsalted butter, at room
    temperature
60 g (2 oz) soft brown sugar
110 g (3½ oz) treacle
1 medium egg, lightly beaten
110 g (3½ oz) almond meal
1 teaspoon baking powder
pinch salt
1 tablespoon ground ginger
¼ teaspoon bicarbonate of soda (baking soda)

Honey Ice Cream

It's best to make the ice cream first. Heat the milk and the vanilla pod and seeds in a saucepan until it is scalding.

In a large bowl, whisk the egg yolks and sugar together until thick and creamy.

Slowly strain the hot milk into the egg mixture, stirring constantly. Transfer the mixture back into a saucepan and heat, stirring constantly until the mixture reaches 80°C (175°F) and thickens. Take off the heat and add the honey and cream.

Cool and churn in an ice cream maker until ice cream forms. Set in the freezer overnight.

Gingerbread with Rhubarb
and Honey Ice Cream (cont.)

Rhubarb

Lay the rhubarb on a baking tin lined with baking paper. Sprinkle over the zest, juice and sugar. Cover with tin foil. Turn the oven up to 180°C (350°F) and bake for 10 minutes.

Gingerbread

Preheat the oven to 170°C (340°F). Grease and line a loaf tin or 12 individual little loaf moulds.

Cream the butter, brown sugar and treacle until light, fluffy and slightly pale. Add the egg gradually, beating well in between each addition.

Sift in the almond meal, baking powder, salt, ground ginger and bicarbonate of soda and fold into the butter mixture.

Pour into a greased loaf tin, or 12 individual moulds. Bake for 30–35 minutes for a loaf or 18–20 minutes for smaller moulds.

The cake will sink in the centre, which creates a nice little bed for the rhubarb, and somewhere for any leftover rhubarb syrup to sit.

To Serve

Serve gingerbread topped with a few pieces of rhubarb, remaining rhubarb syrup and a scoop of honey ice cream.

Licorice Ice Cream with Cherry Syrup

serves 4

350 g (12 oz) eating licorice
400 g (9 oz) thickened cream (35% fat)
4 egg yolks
125 g (4 oz) caster sugar plus one tablespoon
250 g (9 oz) full-fat milk
½ vanilla pod, seeds removed

CHERRY SYRUP
1 jar of morello cherries to get ¼ cup liquid
and ¼ cup cherries, strained

Using a food processor, chop the licorice into small pieces.

Add the licorice to the cream in a medium-sized saucepan and heat on a low heat until simmering. Remove from the heat and leave to infuse for 30 minutes. Reheat again, and let infuse for another 30 minutes. Push the licorice and cream goop through a sieve, to collect the licorice-infused cream.

Meanwhile, make the ice cream base. Beat the egg yolks and 100 g (3½ oz) of the sugar together until light and creamy.

Heat the milk, vanilla seeds and vanilla pod and the remaining sugar together until scalding. Strain, and add the milk to the egg mixture, whisking continuously. Transfer the mixture back into a clean saucepan and put back onto a medium heat and stir continuously until the mixture thickens (between 80–85°C/175–185°F). Remove and let cool. Fold in 250 ml (9 fl oz) of the licorice cream mixture. Strain through a fine sieve and chill.

Transfer to an ice cream machine and churn until set, then transfer to the freezer to freeze hard, about 2 hours.

Cherry Syrup
Open a jar of preserved cherries (these can be your own, or store-bought). Scoop out ¼ cup of cherries and about ½ cup of the liquid. Heat the liquid in a saucepan and reduce down to a syrup. Cool, then add the cherries. Drizzle over scoops of licorice ice cream.

This is so incredibly delicious.

Sun Down

Main Meals

Everyone I know looks forward to dinner. Dinner is a chance to unwind and share your day with those around you. I am lucky that my girlfriends are really good cooks and we share dinner together often. I think that provides me with a lot of inspiration for the following dishes.

Dan and I cook dinner together frequently, which is why some of the dishes here only serve two. But you can easily increase the quantities of ingredients to serve a crowd.

There are dishes here that can be whipped up in a flash, or some that may need more time. There are dishes that require a little technique, or dishes, such as the chicken gratin, that are a simple throw together and bake thing.

I've included some several slow-cooked meals here that will fill your house with amazing smells. The beauty of slow-cooked dishes, is that they can also be whipped up in a fraction of the time (one-third usually) in the pressure cooker. I will try to give you both options here.

Finally, I can't emphasise enough, if you start out with the best quality ingredients, then the cooking part will be easy. And you'll have the most delicious meal to eat too.

Wild fennel is an abundant vegetable you can forage for in cities and in the country. It grows everywhere—along roads, paths or rail tracks. Fennel produces a lovely bulb for roasting or soups; the fronds can be roasted; and the pollen has a strong sweet licorice aroma too. Collect the fennel pollen by placing the wild flowers heads down into a paper bag and shake to remove the pollen. You can also buy pollen from specialty food stores.

Fish in Wild Fennel Pollen, Crispy Potatoes and Wild Sorrel Salad

4 potatoes, peeled and cubed
60 g (2 oz) unsalted butter plus 2 tablespoons
1 handful sorrel leaves
juice of 1 lemon
pinch of salt, to taste
400 g (14 oz) white fish fillet (such as sea bass or snapper)
2 tablespoons wild fennel pollen (foraged or bought)
1 teaspoon salt, or to taste

1 tablespoon olive oil
juice of ½ lemon
fennel bulb fronds, chopped

SALAD
1 radish
1 fennel bulb
chrysanthemum leaves
wild sorrel leaves

Steam or boil the potatoes, until they are soft.

Heat the butter in a frying pan on medium. Fry the potato cubes until crispy. Season with salt to taste. Remove from the heat.

Sprinkle both sides of the fish fillet with pollen and salt (to taste). Heat the olive oil on low heat in a frying pan and place skin-side down. Use a fish slice to put some pressure on the fillets just as they start to fry to prevent their skin from puckering up. Fry the skin side until it is crispy. Flip the fillet over for 30 seconds and then remove.

Add the remaining lemon juice and a knob of butter to the pan and whisk into the juices. Fold in the fennel fronds just before serving.

Finely slice the radish and the fennel. Toss through chrysanthemum leaves and wild sorrel leaves. Drizzle with lemon oil vinaigrette (see basics).

To serve, place the potatoes and salad on the plate and lay the fish fillets on top. Drizzle over with the lemon fennel sauce.

Stuffing a chicken under the skin produces the best breast! I've given you three options, depending on your mood.

- -

Roast Chicken Stuffed Three Ways with Celeriac Purée and Savoy Cabbage

1 whole organic free-range chicken crown
½ lemon
sprig of thyme
sea salt
olive oil
1 fennel bulb, thickly sliced
½ cup white wine
1 cup Brown Chicken Stock (see Basics)
1 tablespoon cream

TRUFFLE STUFFING
1 small truffle
125 g (4 oz) unsalted butter, softened

TARRAGON STUFFING
1 small bunch tarragon leaves
125 g (4 oz) unsalted butter, softened

LEMON STUFFING
125 g (4 oz) unsalted butter, softened
5 thin strips of preserved lemon
juice of ½ lemon
½ lemon cheek

CELERIAC PURÉE
1 tablespoon butter
1 eschalot (shallot), peeled, sliced thinly
1 clove garlic
1 celeriac, chopped into cubes
2 tablespoons thickened cream
salt and pepper, to taste

SAVOY CABBAGE
1 Savoy cabbage
½ cup Vegetable Stock (see Basics)
salt to taste
2 rashers Dry-cured Bacon (see Basics), cut into lardons

Preheat the oven to 200°C (400°F).

Separate the skin from the breast of the chicken by putting your hand at the top of the breast near the neck and rubbing gently under the skin. The skin should come away from the breast quite easily. Remove the wishbone. Now choose a stuffing to place under the skin.

Truffle Stuffing
Grate a quarter of the truffle and mix into the softened butter. Shave the rest of the truffle thinly. With your hand, stuff the truffle butter under the skin of the chicken, and then stuff the slices underneath the skin.

Tarragon Stuffing

Chop the tarragon leaves finely to release their anise flavor. Chop the butter into cubes and mix it with the leaves. Stuff the tarragon butter under the skin.

Lemon Stuffing

Chop the butter into cubes and mix with the preserved lemon. Rub the preserved lemon butter under the skin. Pour the lemon juice in under the skin and rub the lemon cheek over the outside of the skin.

Cooking the Chicken

Once you have stuffed the skin with your choice of stuffing, lay the chicken down and insert ½ a lemon and a sprig of thyme into the cavity. Rub salt over the top of the skin and follow with a drizzle of olive oil.

Place the chicken, breast facing upwards, onto a baking tray. Roast for 45 minutes, basting occasionally with the pan juices. Once golden brown, and the juices run clear, remove from oven, and rest for 5 to 10 minutes.

Celeriac Purée

Heat the butter in a frying pan and sauté the eschalot, garlic and celeriac until warmed through. Cover with water and bring to the boil. Gently simmer for 10 minutes until soft. Transfer to a food processor and blend well for a minute until it is smooth. Add cream to taste and season with salt and pepper.

Savoy Cabbage

Cut the Savoy cabbage in half and cut again into thin wedges about 2 cm (1 in) wide. In a wide pan, bring the vegetable stock to a simmer and lightly braise the cabbage for a few minutes until the cabbage is just soft on each side. Drain the cabbage and set aside. Dry the pan and fry the bacon lardons. Sprinkle them on top of the cabbage.

Finishing the Chicken

Reheat the juices still in the roasting tray on the stovetop. Deglaze the pan with the white wine. Reduce for a few minutes, then add the chicken stock. Bring the mixture to the boil and reduce by half. Strain the sauce, season and pour back into the roasting tray. Add a tablespoon of cream and stir.

Serve rustically in the centre of the table: cabbage, bacon and chicken, with the celeriac purée to the side. Flip a coin to see who gets to carve and enjoy.

Growing up in the country meant that rabbit was often on the table. Here is a wonderful French-inspired dish that will see you coming back for more! The pickled red cabbage goes really well with all meats.

Slow-cooked Rabbit and Burnt Butter Mash with Pickled Red Cabbage

serves 4

1 kg (36 oz) large rabbit
salt and pepper, to taste
300 g (10½ oz) plain (all-purpose) flour
2 tablespoons butter
2 tablespoons olive oil
10 ecshalots (shallots), peeled, roughly chopped
3 cloves garlic, chopped
½ cup white wine
1 tablespoon tomato paste
2 cups Brown Chicken Stock (see Basics)
1 handful thyme, including stalks

BURNT BUTTER MASH

8 Nicola or Maris Piper potatoes, peeled
125 g (4 oz) Beurre Noisette (see Basics)
½ cup full-fat milk, warmed (optional)
salt and pepper, to taste

PICKLED RED CABBAGE

½ red cabbage
1 lemon, juiced
½ cup salt
1 tablespoon white (granulated) sugar, to taste
1 tablespoon butter
½ cup orange juice
2 tablespoons balsamic vinegar

Divide the rabbit into 8 portions or get your butcher to do this for you. Include all the pieces and the bones—it adds the flavour.

Sift the salt, pepper and flour together in a bowl. Dredge the rabbit pieces in the flour.

Preheat the oven to 150°C (300°F).

Heat 1 tablespoon butter and 1 tablespoon oil in a frying pan and brown the rabbit pieces. Transfer to an ovenproof, lidded, casserole dish.

Add another tablespoon each of butter and oil into the pan and sauté the ecshalots for 5 minutes. Add garlic and sauté for another minute. Add to the casserole dish.

A Homegrown Table

Slow-cooked Rabbit and Burnt Butter Mash with Pickled Red Cabbage (cont.)

- -

Pour the white wine, tomato paste and stock to the pan. Stir together for a minute and include all the pan bits.

Pour the liquid over the rabbit in the casserole dish. Sprinkle over a generous handful of thyme, including the stalks. Top up with water at this point to ensure that all of the rabbit is submerged in liquid. Cover and place in the oven for approximately 2 hours. At this point you could also choose to cook the rabbit in a pressure cooker and cook at pressure for about 40 minutes.

To prepare the cabbage, finely slice the cabbage and toss through the salt (this may seem like a lot but you will be rinsing it off). Set aside for 40–60 minutes. Rinse off the salt. Bring a pot of water to the boil, and drop rinsed cabbage into the boiling water and blanch for one minute and then refresh in cold water. Strain and put into Pickling Liquid (see Basics).

Meanwhile, place the whole potatoes in a saucepan, cover with water and bring to the boil. Cook the potatoes until soft—about 30 minutes. Mash finely or pass through a sieve. Stir the beurre noisette through, then add the warmed milk, if using. Season with salt and pepper and keep warm.

Serve the rabbit in wide-lipped bowls. Spoon the mash on the bottom and add the rabbit. Place some pickled cabbage on the side.

These are not your ordinary meatballs—they are amazing meatballs that my friend Jo created. They are really fresh, herby and zesty. Everybody who has tried these loves them.

Pork and Fennel Meatballs with Risoni

serves 4

600 g (21 oz) pork mince
3 teaspoons fennel seeds
1 onion, very finely chopped
2 eggs, beaten
100 g (3½ oz) fine breadcrumbs
zest of 1 lemon
¼ cup parmesan cheese, grated, plus extra, shaved for serving
salt and pepper, to season
olive oil
2 cloves garlic, finely chopped

1 x 400 g (14 oz) jar passata sauce (tomato purée)
salt and pepper, to taste
1 tablespoon balsamic vinegar
2 cups stock
4 cups water
1 cup risoni
1 tablespoon butter
1 bunch fresh flat-leaf parsley, chopped
zest of 1 lemon
½ lemon, juiced

Combine the pork mince, fennel seeds, onion, eggs, breadcrumbs, lemon zest, parmesan, and salt and pepper in a bowl. Use your hands to mix well together. Shape into small balls, no bigger than a golf ball.

Heat the olive oil in a frying pan and brown the balls on the outside. Set aside on some kitchen paper to drain. Keep the olive oil in the pan.

Brown the garlic cloves in the oil and pour in the jar of passata. Add salt and pepper, and vinegar and bring to a simmer. Add the sautéed pork balls to the sauce and simmer for 30 minutes.

In a saucepan, add the stock and water and bring to the boil. Pour in the risoni and the butter and simmer for 10 minutes. Strain. Toss in shaves of parmesan along with most of the parsley, lemon zest and juice.

Divide the risoni among the serving bowls, with the meatballs on the top. Decorate with a few remaining shavings of parmesan and remaining parsley.

Sun Down

My lovely friend Lynton says this is a delicious way to cook lamb. This recipe uses the sous vide technique to cook the lamb perfectly.

- -

Lamb Rack with Olive Tapenade and Broadbean, Pea and Chickweed Salad

8 point lamb rack, halved into 4 portions
1 tablespoon olive oil, plus extra for frying
2 bay leaves
sprig of rosemary
2 sprigs of thyme

OLIVE TAPENADE
120 g (4 oz) pitted black olives
1 teaspoon capers
1 anchovy
1 teaspoon thyme leaves
1 small clove garlic
2 tablespoons extra virgin olive oil
1 teaspoon lemon juice
1 small bunch flat-leaf parsley
freshly ground black pepper

BROAD BEAN SALAD
2 pinches salt
300 g (10½ oz) broad beans, shelled and skinned
200 g (7 oz) shelled fresh peas
2 large tomatoes, peeled, de-seeded and finely diced
1 tablespoon olive oil
handful of chickweed tips
2 teaspoons lemon juice
salt and pepper, to taste

fried saltbush, to serve

Trim the fat off the lamb rack, leaving only a thin layer. Place each lamb portion into a sous vide bag, or a ziplock bag, and add olive oil and herbs. Seal the bags and place in a water bath or saucepan filled with water for 1 hour at 60°C (140°F). Alternatively, you can cook in a hot frying pan with a drizzle of olive oil, flipping every few minutes until nice and brown, and then putting into a 180°C (350°F) oven for 10 minutes. Rest.

Make the olive tapenade by pulsing all the ingredients in a food processor. Don't over-blend—keep it coarse.

To prepare the broad beans, bring 1 litre (36 fl oz) of water to the boil in a saucepan. Add 2 pinches of salt and blanch the broad beans and peas for 1 minute. Remove and plunge into cold water.

Lamb Rack with Olive Tapenade and Broadbean, Pea and Chickweed Salad (cont.)

Place the tomatoes in a bowl with a dash of olive oil. Add the beans and peas and stir.

Remove the lamb racks from the sous vide bags.

Heat the extra olive oil in a frying pan over a high heat and quickly sear each side of the lamb racks. Turn regularly so they do not cook through. Remove the lamb and let it rest for 5 minutes. While it is resting, smear with the olive tapenade. Keep the pan juices. Cut each lamb rack into individual cutlets.

Place the broad bean salad, except for the chickweed, in the frying pan with the juices. Toss in the tablespoon of oil and a squeeze of lemon juice, salt and pepper and stir for a minute. Remove from the heat and spoon the broad bean salad on to the serving plates. Spoon the broad bean salad on the serving plates and top with chickweed. Garnish with pan-fried saltbush and lay the cutlets on top.

Note: Sous vide involves cooking food in airtight plastic bags, submerged in a water bath, at a regulated temperature. The temperature for cooking is much lower than normal-typically around 55°C (130°F) to 60°C (140°F) for meat and slightly higher for vegetables. This method allows you to cook the item evenly, without overcooking and still keeping the inside perfectly cooked.

This is a great way to prepare a roast chicken. One chicken ballotine gives about eight slices, which serves about four and ensures that everyone gets a piece of leg and a piece of breast—now that's fair!

- -

Chicken Ballotine with Preserved Lemon and Bread Stuffing

serves 4

1 whole free-range chicken
20 cm (8 in) French bread stick/baguette
¼ preserved lemon, skin only, rinsed and finely chopped
1 egg, beaten
1 clove garlic, finely chopped

1 teaspoon thyme leaves
sea salt and freshly cracked black pepper, to taste
1 tablespoon olive oil
40 g (1½ oz) Clarified Butter (see Basics)
salt and pepper, to taste

Preheat the oven to 160°C (320°F).

Debone the chicken completely or ask your butcher if you don't know how to do this.

Crumb the bread stick in a food processor. In a bowl, mix the breadcrumbs, preserved lemon, egg, garlic, thyme, salt, pepper and olive oil. Blend with your hands to make a stuffing.

Lay the chicken out flat on a bench with the skin side down. Roll the stuffing into a log and place it down the centre of the chicken (where the spine was) and truss with string (see diagram below).

Pat the outside of the chicken with butter, salt and pepper.

Place the chicken in a baking tin with olive oil and bake for 45–60 minutes or until the juices run clear (or the centre of the chicken reads 65°C (150°F) on a meat thermometer.

Serve this with crispy potatoes, a simple green salad, or the Broadbean, Pea and Chickweed Salad (see recipe page 170).

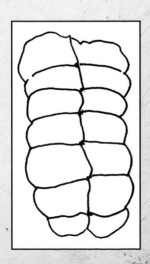

Sun Down

This is my go-to comfort dish—when I am lucky enough to get a rib eye from my parents' farm. They are so delicious—they go quick!

Rib Eye with Bordelaise Sauce, Crispy Potato Skins and Watercress Salad

6 large Sebago potatoes
1 cup vegetable oil
salt, to taste
olive oil, to drizzle
2 regular rib eye steaks, about 4 cm
    (2 in) thick

WATERCRESS SALAD
1 bunch watercress
¼ cup Basic Vinaigrette (see Basics)

BORDELAISE SAUCE
1 bunch of tarragon
60 ml (2 fl oz) white wine vinegar
120 ml (4 fl oz) water
1 eschalot (shallot), peeled, thinly sliced
4 peppercorns
1 bay leaf
3 egg yolks
200 g (7 oz) Clarified Butter (see Basics)
½ lemon, juiced

Preheat the oven to 180°C (350°F).

Scrub the potatoes and peel off the skin. Deep-fry the skins in 1 cup of vegetable oil heated to 180°C (350°F) in a saucepan. Once crisp, remove with a slotted spoon. Salt to taste.

Rub salt and olive oil into the steak. Heat the griddle pan to very hot (smoking) and pan-fry the steaks for 6–8 minutes on each side, turning only once. This is for a medium rare result for a 4 cm (2 in) thick steak. Use less time if your steak is thinner, or more if your steak is thicker. Let your steak rest for at least 5–10 minutes before serving.

To make the bordelaise sauce, strip the leaves from the tarragon and set to one side. Put the tarragon stalks, vinegar, water, eschalot, peppercorns and bay leaf in a small saucepan and boil until the liquid is reduced by half—about 10 minutes.

Rib Eye with Bordelaise Sauce, Crispy Potato Skins and Watercress Salad (cont.)

Pour 2 tablespoons of this liquid (there may be some left over, reserve for another day) into a bowl with 2 tablespoons water. Add the egg yolks and whisk together. Place this bowl over a double boiler and whisk until the mixture is thick and creamy—about 5 minutes.

Warm the Clarified Butter. Very slowly pour this into the egg yolk mixture, whisking continuously to form an emulsion. Remove from the double boiler.

Chop the reserved tarragon leaves and add to the finished sauce. If it is too thick add warm water; if it is too thin, add more clarified butter. Turn the heat down to keep warm.

Make a simple watercress salad. Tear the bunch of watercress into a bowl and toss through White Wine Vinaigrette.

Remove rib eye from the oven and rest for at least 5 minutes (you can rest in a warm place for up to 40 minutes).

To serve, slice the rib eye off the bone into pieces 2 cm (1 in) wide across the grain and divide among the plates. Arrange with watercress salad and potato skins on the plate. Pour the sauce over the steak.

Fat hen is a foraged leaf, similar to spinach or kale. It grows all over the world and has a very earthy taste and becomes crispy when you dry fry it. I like to add Hung Yoghurt to this recipe, making it nice and creamy. This recipe just calls for the loins of rabbit. Use the rest of your rabbit in the Slow-cooked Rabbit and Burnt Butter Mash with Pickled Red Cabbage (see recipe page 164).

Pancetta-wrapped Rabbit with Fat Hen and Wild Blackberry Sauce

2 cups chicken stock
½ cup barley
2 rabbit loins
salt and pepper, to season
6 long thin, belly slices of pancetta
caul fat (ask your butcher for this)
olive oil, to fry
1 teaspoon caster (superfine) sugar
2 tablespoons Raspberry Vinegar (see Basics)
handful wild blackberries

2 tablespoons water
salt, to taste
1 bunch fat hen
1 tablespoon olive oil
4 tablespoons Hung Yoghurt (see Basics)

In a medium-sized saucepan, bring the chicken stock to the boil and pour in the barley. Cook until just tender, for approximately 30 minutes.

Remove the loins from the rabbit, or ask your butcher to do this. Season with salt and pepper. Press the loins together, with opposite ends facing, to make a nice evenly sized sausage shape.

Set out a large piece of cling film. Lay the pancetta slices out so they overlap onto the cling film in a row. Place the loins across the slices.

Pick up the cling film and roll the loin into the pancetta slices and squeeze it together to form a nice sausage. The pancetta should cover the rabbit once and the pancetta fat will help this to stick together. Trim off any excess pancetta. Refrigerate for 5 minutes.

Pancetta-wrapped Rabbit with Fat Hen and Wild Blackberry Sauce (cont.)

Remove the plastic from the rabbit. Trim the caul fat to a 30 cm (12 in) square and wrap around the rabbit sausage. Heat a pan to medium hot with a teaspoon of olive oil. Pan-fry the rabbit sausage carefully turning it on each side for 6–8 minutes—it cooks quite quickly. Remove the sausage from the pan and set aside to rest.

Using the same pan, shake in the caster sugar and melt it in the pancetta juices. Add the Raspberry Vinegar, blackberries and water, and reduce. Season with salt and leave on a low heat.

While the sauce is reducing, drain the barley.

Heat another saucepan with 1 tablespoon of olive oil and toss the fat hen leaves for about 20 seconds until they crisp up.

Slice the rabbit loin into 2 cm (1 in) chunks.

To serve, spoon a portion of the yoghurt on each plate and sprinkle over the barley. Top with the rabbit slices. Sprinkle the fat hen on the plate and spoon over the warm blackberry sauce.

Fresh tastes of the sea come together in this simple dish. Samphire and sea spinach is foraged from the sea shore and is now becoming a common ingredient in markets.

- -

Crispy-skinned Fish with Pippis and Sea Herbs

2 large tomatoes
6 baby chat potatoes
olive oil, to fry
2 x 200 g (7 oz) white fish fillets

1 large bunch samphire and/or pigface leaves
200 g (7 oz) pippis or clams
½ lemon, juiced

Score the base of the tomatoes and blanch the tomatoes in hot water for about 30 seconds. Peel and cut into quarters. Remove fleshy seeds and discard. Dice the remaining flesh.

Put the potatoes in a pot of cold salted water and bring to the boil slowly.

Heat a pan with olive oil to medium. Place the fish skin-side down. Use a fish slice to put some pressure on the fillets just as they start to fry, to prevent their skin from puckering up. Fry the fish slowly to crisp up the skin.

Flip the fish over for 10–15 seconds and remove.

Into that fishy pan, throw the samphire, pigface and pippis.

Add the lemon juice and steam the pippis open. Throw in the tomatoes and stir.

Serve the tender potatoes with the fish, pippis, sea herbs and pan juices. Yum—so fresh and delicious.

The lamb I eat is often raised on saltbush, a hardy bush that adds a distinct flavour to the meat. If you can get saltbush lamb, this is ideal for this dish. Saltbush is also used as a herb for cooking. You can substitute with rosemary, but the taste will be a little different.

Eight-hour Lamb

1 kg (36 oz) lamb shoulder, sliced (ask your
 butcher to do this for you)
½ cup plain (all-purpose) flour, for dusting
2 tablespoons sea salt
2 tablespoons olive oil
1 bunch thyme
2 bay leaves
2 sprigs rosemary
1 garlic bulb, peeled and chopped
2 onions, peeled and sliced

2 carrots, washed and chopped
2 sticks of celery, chopped
1 star anise
1 lemon, juiced
1 tablespoon butter
saltbush, to serve

Preheat the oven to 90°C (195°F).

Dust the lamb in the plain flour and sea salt. Heat a frying pan with the olive oil and brown off the lamb pieces. Put the pieces of lamb into a heavy casserole dish, with a lid.

Place the remaining ingredients into the casserole dish with the lamb, and mix together with your hands. Cover the lamb entirely with water, ensuring the lamb is submerged by 3 cm (about 1 in).

Cling film the top of the casserole dish and then place lid on the top. Cook for 8 hours.

To make crispy fried saltbush, heat a little oil in a saucepan over medium-high and toss in the salt bush for 20–30 seconds until crispy.

Serve with creamy mash and crispy fried saltbush.

Oxtail is delicious and, in my opinion, has an even better flavour than osso bucco. I urge you to try it.

Braised Oxtail with Gremolata and Polenta

serves 4

OXTAIL BRAISE
1 oxtail, cut into 8 pieces
1 tablespoon oil, for frying
2 cups Brown Chicken Stock (see Basics),
    to cover
1 carrot, chopped
½ leek, chopped
1 onion, peeled and chopped
4 cloves garlic, chopped
1 stalk celery, chopped
4 fresh tomatoes, chopped
1 cup red wine
few sprigs of thyme
2 bay leaves
1 teaspoon peppercorns
1 star anise

CREAMY POLENTA
2 cups full-fat milk
2 cups water
1 cup polenta
1 tablespoon butter
¼ cup shaved parmesan

GREMOLATA
bunch of flat-leaf parsley, finely chopped
small slice of preserved lemon rind, finely
    chopped
zest of ½ lemon
1 clove garlic, finely chopped

Sear the oxtail pieces in a hot pan with 1 tablespoon of oil until browned on all sides. Transfer to a pressure cooker and add the remaining ingredients for the oxtail braise. Cook at pressure for 45 minutes. After 45 minutes, turn off the heat and let pressure subside. Remove lid from pressure cooker and, with a slotted spoon, remove oxtail pieces. Heat the remaining sauce and simmer, reducing by half. Once reduced, strain through a sieve. Return the oxtail pieces to the strained sauce. Set aside.

To make the polenta, bring the milk and the water together in a large saucepan to a boil. Add the polenta very gradually, whisking continuously. Reduce heat to low and cook, stirring with a wooden spoon, for 5–6 minutes until thick. Take off the heat and stir in the butter and parmesan.

Mix the gremolata ingredients together in a bowl and set aside.

To serve, spoon polenta out on individual plates, place oxtail pieces on top, and sprinkle with gremolata. So comforting.

Sun Down

Pork cheeks are delicious. With some love in preparation and cooking, you will enjoy beautiful, flavoursome soft pork.

Pork Cheeks with Char-grilled Fennel and Burnt Fennel Fronds

serves 4

4 pork cheeks
2 x 330 ml (11½ fl oz) bottles apple cider
500 ml (17½ fl oz) water
2 star anise
1 tablespoon licorice root
1 stalk celery, chopped

1 carrot, chopped
1 onion, peeled and chopped
2 cloves garlic, chopped
2 sprigs thyme
2 fennel bulbs, tops removed, fennels quartered
olive oil, to brush on fennel bulbs

Braise the pork cheeks and everything listed above, except for the fennel bulbs, in a pressure cooker. Cook at pressure for 1½ hours. After this time, remove from the heat and let it cool to enable you to remove the lid. If you are not using a pressure cooker, put all of the above ingredients into a large casserole dish, cover the top with aluminium foil, and place a lid on the top. Cook submerged cheeks in the oven at 160°C (320°F) for 4–4½ hours. Carefully remove the cheeks from the braising liquid and gently simmer the liquid until reduced by half. Pat dry the cheeks.

Preheat the oven to 200°C (400°F).

Place the pork cheeks onto a lined baking tray. Place fennel fronds onto another baking tray lined with baking paper.

Put both trays into the oven and cook for 8–10 minutes. Remove pork cheeks. By this time, the fennel should be black and burnt. If not, keep in the oven until it is. Trust me, burnt fennel fronds taste awesome.

Meanwhile, heat a griddle pan to hot. Brush the fennel quarters with oil and char-grill.

To serve, plate 2 quarters of fennel and a pork cheek on a plate. Drizzle with sauce and garnish with the burnt fennel.

Beef cheeks and vanilla—a perfect match!

Beef Cheeks with Vanilla

serves 4

*2 tablespoons plain (all-purpose) flour,
combined with 1 teaspoon each of salt and
pepper*
4 beef cheeks
4 tablespoons olive oil
1 stalk celery, diced
1 carrot, diced
2 eschalots (shallots), finely chopped
6 cloves garlic, chopped
1 cup port

1 vanilla pod, split and seeds scraped
dash of cognac
1 teaspoon peppercorns
2 cardamom pods, crushed
2 fresh bay leaves
1 litre (36 fl oz) Simple Stock (see Basics)
1 tablespoon tomato paste
1 tablespoon sherry vinegar

Preheat the oven to 150°C (300°F). Sift the flour mixture onto a plate. Pat dry the beef cheeks and toss them in the seasoned flour, shaking off any excess.

Heat 2 tablespoons of olive oil in a medium-sized saucepan and fry the beef cheeks on each side until the meat is brown.

Transfer the cheeks into a cast-iron casserole dish. Sauté the celery, carrot, eschalots and garlic with another 2 tablespoons of oil in the same saucepan that the beef cheeks were fried in. Deglaze with the port and pour the mixture into the casserole with the beef cheeks.

Add in the remaining ingredients, including the vanilla pod and seeds. Add extra water to cover, if required. Place a cartouche (see How to make a cartouche page 131) on the surface of the beef cheeks.

Cover with foil, then with a lid and cook for 3–4 hours. Alternatively, put in a pressure cooker (without the cartouche) and cook at pressure for 1½ hours.

Remove the beef cheeks and reduce the remaining sauce down by half.

Serve with a side of mashed turnips and swedes, some lightly sautéed kale and sauce.

Mum loves these so much! She actually made the ribs in the photo. These ribs are delicious, sticky and great with a beer. The recipe makes ample barbecue sauce, so you could probably get away with adding more ribs—it's up to you".

Sticky Beef Ribs

serves 4

4 beef ribs, cut across the ribs with 3 ribs per portion.

BARBECUE SAUCE
2 cups homemade tomato sauce (see Basics, alternatively, use a store-bought tomato sauce or ketchup)
1 onion, finely diced
8 cloves garlic, finely diced
½ cup oil (any variety is fine)
½ cup maple syrup
½ cup brown sugar

1 tablespoon apple cider vinegar
1 tablespoon tomato paste
1 tablespoon Worcestershire sauce
1 chipotle chilli, finely chopped
4 teaspoons smoked paprika
1 teaspoon dry mustard powder
½ teaspoon cayenne pepper
zest and juice of one orange
⅓ cup smoky whiskey
4 teaspoons sea salt
good grind black pepper

To prepare the ribs, bring a large pot of salted water to the boil. Simmer the ribs, submerged in the water for 2 hours until soft. Allow the ribs to cool in the water.

Preheat the oven to 180°C (350°F).

To prepare the sauce, combine all of the barbecue sauce ingredients in a medium-sized saucepan and bring to a boil and then simmer on a low heat for 20 minutes or until thick.

Drain the ribs from the water and smear them generously with the sauce. Place the beef ribs bone side down in a roasting tray and roast for 1 hour.

Serve with Pink Coleslaw with Horseradish (see recipe page 102), some Pickled Red Cabbage (see recipe page 164), or some Pickled Red Onion (see Basics) and eat with happiness.

Hangar steak is a cut of beef from around the diaphragm. Cooked rare to medium rare, it is a delicious and quick cut to cook. It has a beautiful flavour and goes well with the simplest of accompaniments. It is best to trim the steak of any sinew and fat so you have a uniform shape to cook, as the brief cooking time does not allow time to render fat. You should not overcook this, otherwise it is tough and inedible. Also great served with Wild Green Salad (see page 83), Chipotle Mayonnaise (see page 101) and Yoghurt Flat Bread (see page 76).

Hangar Steak with Eschalot Purée, Roast Eschalots and Pickled Eschalots with Horseradish

serves 4

1 teaspoon mustard seeds
¼ cup white wine vinegar
¼ cup honey
¼ water
10 banana eschalots (shallots), peeled
150 g (5 oz) pine mushrooms, thinly sliced, or other mushrooms in season

1 tablespoon olive oil, plus extra for roasting
salt and pepper, to taste
4 hangar steaks, about 160 g (5½ oz) each
2 tablespoons olive oil, for frying
5 cm (2 in) piece horseradish
2 handfuls young baby beet leaves

To make the pickled eschalots, toast the mustard seeds by dry frying them in a heavy-based saucepan. Add the vinegar, honey and water. Bring to the boil and remove from the heat. Slice 2 eschalots and add to vinegar honey pickling solution. Slice the mushrooms and add to the eschalots. They can pickle happily together. Set aside until needed.

To make the eschalot purée, heat 1 tablespoon of olive oil in the same saucepan. Finely chop 4 eschalots and sauté them in the oil until soft and translucent. Transfer to a food processor and blend until smooth. Season.

To make the roast eschalots, preheat the oven to 175°C (345°F). Slice the remaining eschalots in half, drizzle with oil and roast in the oven for 30 minutes. Remove eschalots from the oven.

Heat 1 tablespoon of olive oil in a cast-iron frying pan on a very high heat. Season and fry the steaks on each side for about 1 minute, depending on the thickness. It is very important not to overcook.

Remove the steaks from the pan and rest for 5 minutes. Then slice across the grain.

To serve, smear the eschalot purée on each plate and arrange 2 roast eschalot halves on top. Place slices of hangar steak over the eschalots, top with the pickled eschalots and mushrooms. Grate horseradish over the top and sprinkle with baby beet leaves.

Sun Down

Simple and tasty. Fun to make and easy to eat.

Nettle Ravioli and Goat's Cheese

serves 4

Fresh Pasta for 4 people (see Basics)
½ eschalot (shallot), peeled and thinly sliced
1 clove garlic, peeled and chopped
1 tablespoon butter
400 g (14 oz) nettle leaves, removed from
 stalks (be careful and wear gloves while the
 nettles are fresh, when they are cooked their
 sting has gone)

olive oil
salt and pepper, to taste
150 g (5 oz) goat's cheese, crumbled

Make a quantity of pasta dough for 4 people. Divide the dough into 2 portions and roll out 2 lengths of pasta sheets on the thinnest setting. Set aside.

In a deep saucepan, sauté the eschalot and garlic in butter. Add the nettles and sauté until fully wilted—about 4 minutes. Add 2 tablespoons of water to help steam the nettles. Place the mixture in a food processor and pulse it to a coarse paste. Season with salt and pepper.

Lay out one sheet of pasta. Dollop teaspoons of nettle paste across the pasta about 8 cm (4 in) apart. Brush with water around each dollop of purée. Working quickly, use a cookie cutter to cut out enough lids from the other pasta sheet. Place a lid on top of each nettle dollop. Press down around each dollop to remove the air and to sandwich the pasta sheets together. Using a slightly smaller cookie cutter, cut the ravioli out, and place on a lightly floured baking tray. Repeat with the remaining ravioli. If you don't have cookie cutters, you can cut squares of pasta with a knife.

Bring a deep saucepan of salted water to the boil. Cook the ravioli in the water until they float to the top. Remove the cooked ravioli using a slotted spoon, place in a bowl and toss in olive oil and salt and pepper, to stop them sticking together.

Crumble the fresh goat's cheese over the top and serve. Simply delicious.

Sun Down

Ahh, the smell of summer!

- -

Barbecued Quail With Heirloom Tomato Salad

serves 4

4 quail, spatchcocked
1 tablespoon fennel seeds, toasted
1 tablespoon coriander seeds, toasted
2 cloves garlic
½ teaspoon peppercorns
½ handful tarragon
1 handful continental parsley

zest and juice of 1 lemon
¼ cup olive oil
4 heirloom tomatoes, sliced
1 tablespoon sherry vinegar
salt, to taste
1 tablespoon olive oil

Spatchcock the quail, by cutting the backbone out with scissors, and squashing the bird out flat, or ask the butcher to do this for you.

In a mortar and pestle, pound the fennel seeds, coriander seeds, garlic and peppercorns together. Add the tarragon, then the parsley, then the lemon zest and juice and the olive oil. Smear the marinade mixture over the quails and let them marinate for at least 30 minutes or overnight.

Turn on the barbecue. Using the grill, turn the barbecue to high and cook the quails for about 4 minutes each side.

Dress the sliced tomatoes with the sherry vinegar, salt and olive oil.

To serve, place some tomatoes on each plate and top with a barbecued quail. This dish also goes very well with the Char-grilled Vegetables with Nettle Pesto (see page 75).

A Homegrown Table

This is incredibly easy and incredibly delicious! It is the ultimate busy person's comfort food. You can brown the chicken pieces off in a pan before adding them to the other ingredients, or, as noted here, just put everything in together. It just depends how much time you have.

- -

Chicken Gratin and Salt-baked Potatoes

serves 4

1 chicken, cut into 10–12 pieces (ask your butcher to cut the chicken into pieces)
2 eschalots (shallots), finely chopped
2 cloves garlic, finely chopped
1 stalk celery, finely diced
2 tablespoons thyme leaves
2 bay leaves
400 ml (14 fl oz) white wine, such as Riesling
400 ml (14 fl oz) Brown Chicken Stock (see Basics)
80 g (2½ oz) parmesan, finely grated
1 cup fresh breadcrumbs

olive oil, to drizzle
6 egg whites
150 g (5 oz) salt
100 ml (3½ fl oz) water
500 g (17½ oz) plain (all-purpose) flour
4 medium potatoes, scrubbed
Easy Awesome bread, to serve (optional see basics)
½ bunch Cavalo Nero, centre seam removed.
1 tablespoon olive oil
Homemade Butter (see Basics)

Preheat the oven to 180°C (350°F).

Season chicken with salt. Place in a large bowl and add the eschalots, garlic, celery, thyme and bay leaves. Mix well to combine.

Place chicken mixture into a large 2-litre pie dish (or 4 x 400 ml/14 fl oz pie dishes). Pour over white wine and the chicken stock, ensuring all pieces of chicken are covered by liquid. Add more stock if required. Sprinkle over parmesan, breadcrumbs and drizzle with olive oil (in that order). Place onto a large tray and bake for 1 hour, until the chicken falls off the bone.

For the salt crust dough, mix egg whites, salt, water and flour in bowl to form a dough. Divide dough into four, then roll into balls. Roll dough balls out, large enough to enclose potatoes. Place a potato into the centre of each piece of dough, and wrap up to enclose, ensuring the potato is completely encased. Place potatoes onto a tray and bake for 1 hour.

To sauté the cavalo nero, heat 1 tablespoon oil in a pan and toss through cavalo nero until just wilted. To serve, place some gratin plates. Place a potato on the side. Serve with crusty bread and cavalo nero.

Sun Down

Basics

Recipes from My Pantry

The following section contains some of my tried and true chutneys, preserves, pastries and techniques. There are hints and tips here to ensure you can make your food really special.

Homemade jam on homemade bread will make you happy. A rough puff pastry can be quite easy and is better than the bought stuff. You can smoke your own salmon and cure your own bacon. Smoking your own salmon allows you to create a beautiful product rom a simple salmon fillet. Now you can have your own free-range bacon, just by curing some free range pork belly.Beurre noisette is simple but adds so much depth of flavour to your cooking. Homemade bread is simply the best, and only has four ingredients—one of those is water. Go berry picking in berry season and make enough jam for the year. Turn your glut of tomatoes into tomato kasundi (or eggplant). Don't even get me started on quince paste. Those who know me know that I will supply the quince paste at every opportunity. It keeps so well and is so delicious. This section emphasises real food and how you can make real food easily, and often much more affordably than pre-prepared. And all the recipes are so very satisfying to make.

Homemade Butter and Buttermilk

300 ml (10½ fl oz) cream makes
100 ml (3½ fl oz) buttermilk and approx. 200 g (7 oz) butter

Put the cream into your stand mixer and whisk until the liquid separates (about 5 minutes)—you can't overbeat this!

If in doubt process for a few more minutes. Pour off the liquid at the bottom of the processor—this is the buttermilk! The solid is butter—how easy is that?

Pat the butter dry with paper towel.

Beurre Noisette

I use this all the time in my recipes and each time I am amazed by its wonderful nutty flavour.

150 g (5 oz) unsalted butter

Chop the butter into cubes. Melt the butter in a saucepan and bring to a boil, stirring—it will be quite noisy and will start to foam on the top.

Continue to boil for approximately 2 minutes as the bubbles get bigger. Keep a watch on the saucepan. The big bubbles will disappear and the butter will darken. Once the bubbling stops and the butter starts to catch on the bottom remove from the heat to stop it from cooking. It will have a light syrupy consistency and smell nutty.

A Homegrown Table

Smoked Butter

wood chips (or smoking shavings)
ice cubes

250 g (9 oz) butter, chopped into
2 cm (1 in) cubes

Prepare the smoking kit. I use my stainless steel saucepan, lined with foil, with a steamer insert and lid. You will also need a small saucer that fits loosely into the steamer insert, to allow the smoke to get through.

Dry fry a handful of wood shavings in a separate heavy cast-iron frying pan (don't use a non-stick pan for this, you may ruin it). Put the frying pan on as high a heat as you can. Do not leave this pan alone!

While doing that, put a saucer into the steamer insert and put ice cubes on top of the saucer. Place the butter on top of the ice cubes and put the lid on the steamer insert to seal it. Cling film the lid onto the steamer insert to seal it.

After 3–4 minutes the smoke from the chips will be intense (I even wait for mine to catch on fire but only do this if you feel confident). Transfer the smoking chips into the foil-lined saucepan and place the prepared steamer on top and cling film the lid of the steamer insert to the saucepan to create an airtight smoker.

Leave for 20–30 minutes. If you want to double-smoke the butter, repeat the entire smoking process.

Clarified Butter

Clarify the butter by heating it in the microwave for a minute or heating it in a saucepan on the stovetop for a few minutes.

Melt gently so that the solids sink to the bottom. You want the golden liquid on the top only. Do not boil as the bubbling will mix the solids and liquids together.

Pour off the golden liquid and discard the solids. If you don't need it immediately, store the clarified butter in the fridge. It will keep for up to a month.

Hung Yoghurt

500 ml (17 fl oz) plain natural yoghurt

Place plain natural yoghurt into a sieve lined with a muslin cloth. Place the sieve over a bowl and place in the refrigerator. Ideally, strain for 12–24 hours, but I have found that even after an hour, you can achieve a thicker yoghurt.

I make this bread all the time. Everyone who eats this is amazed at how easy it is to make and how awesome it tastes—easy, awesome bread!

Easy Awesome Bread

500 g (17½ oz) plain (all-purpose) flour, sifted
2 teaspoons dry yeast
2 teaspoons salt
350 ml (12 fl oz) warm water, up to 60°C (122°F)

In a large bowl, mix the dry ingredients together. Make a well in the flour and pour in the water. Using an electric mixer with a dough hook attachment, or your hands, knead for 5–10 minutes. Cover the dough with a tea towel and leave it to prove in a warm draught-free spot for one hour or until doubled in size (sometimes, in winter, I turn my oven on the lowest setting and put the dough in there, leaving the oven door open).

Divide the dough into two portions and then shape each loaf into two round balls. Alternatively, place into greased loaf tins. Place onto baking paper-lined trays and leave to prove for another 30 minutes.

Preheat the oven to 200°C (400°F).

Score an incision at least 2 cm deep across the top of each loaf with a knife, and dust with extra flour.

Bake for 25–30 minutes until golden brown. The bread is ready when it sounds hollow on the bottom when you tap it. Aim for a nice dark brown crust.

Buns in (almost) under an hour! I have taken a few shortcuts in this recipe and have found that the buns come out just as well. These are wonderful buns to serve as sliders with pulled pork and coleslaw on the side. They are also lovely with sticky beef ribs. You can add some sultanas as well and have lovely sultana buns. They are great on their own with homemade jam and butter—so versatile.

Slider Milk Buns with Wild Fennel Seeds

60 g (2 oz) unsalted butter
250 ml (9 fl oz) full-fat milk
7 g (one sachet) dry yeast
500 g (17½ oz) strong bread flour
40 g (1½ oz) caster (superfine) sugar

2 teaspoons salt
2 large eggs, lightly beaten
1 egg, whisked for wash
wild fennel seeds

Add the butter to the milk and warm until the butter melts—but don't take the temperature past 60°C (140°F).

Using an electric mixer with a dough hook attachment, mix the dry ingredients together, then pour in the warmed milk mixture. Add the beaten eggs. Knead with dough hook for 5 minutes, until stretchy. You can also do this by hand—knead the dough on a flour-free bench for 10–15 minutes.

Shape into 100 g (3½ oz) balls of dough rolling it with your cupped palm, on the bench. Prove in a warm place.

Preheat the oven to 200°C (400°F).

Brush the buns with egg wash and sprinkle liberally with fennel seeds.

Bake for 10–15 minutes until dark golden. Remove from the oven and leave to cool on a wire rack.

Rough Puff Pastry

225 g (8 oz) plain (all-purpose) flour, sifted
225 g (8 oz) unsalted butter, chopped
125 ml (4 fl oz) ice cold water
¼ teaspoon salt

To make the rough puff pastry, put the flour on the bench and make a well. Put the chopped butter into the well. Using a pastry scraper, chop the butter into the flour and salt and combine.

Make a well in the flour mixture again. Pour in 100 ml (3½ fl oz) of the cold water. Mix into the dough slowly to form a ball. The dough should be firm but pliable—don't worry if you still have chunks of butter visible. Roll the pastry into a rectangle (see the step photos to the left, where Dan is my lovely hand model. This was his first time making rough puff!).

Fold each end into the middle like a book (photo 2), and then close the pastry again (photo 3–5). Wrap the dough in cling film and put in the fridge for 20 minutes. Roll out into a rectangle and fold over into itself again. Cover and refrigerate for 20 minutes. Repeat this step one more time.

Leave in the refrigerator until ready for use. You can also freeze this for up to 3 months.

Basics

219

I love making fresh pasta. Once you learn how to make it and with a bit of practise, you have a great food skill for life. Making pasta is about proportions, so I am going to give you proportions and then you can work it out—I promise it'll turn out okay!

Fresh Pasta

FOR EACH PERSON:
100 g (3½ oz) flour ('00' is best)
1 egg yolk
½ teaspoon oil
½ teaspoon water (optional, depending on the flour)

TO MAKE ENOUGH PASTA FOR FOUR PEOPLE YOU NEED:
400 g (14 oz) flour
4 eggs
2 teaspoons olive oil
2 teaspoons water

It's best to mix pasta by hand; you get a much better feel for the pasta dough. Pour the flour onto a workbench and make a well in the centre. Crack the eggs into the centre of the well. Pour in the oil. Break the eggs up with your fingers and then start incorporating the flour in from the sides. Continue to do this until you have a rough dough.

Knead the dough for about 10 minutes until a soft, smooth dough forms. If it is too wet, add some flour and if it is too dry, add a few drops of water.

Cover the dough in cling film and rest it out of the fridge for 30 minutes. Get your pasta machine out and attach it firmly to the bench.

Divide the dough into two pieces. Work one piece at a time and keep the other one covered. Set the pasta machine to the largest/widest setting. Gently feed the dough through the machine. Repeat. Fold the dough in half and feed through the machine again. Repeat. Fold in half again and repeat this process seven times.

If the pasta gets a little bit sticky in this process you can dust with some flour. This is laminating the pasta and it will ensure that the pasta holds together while cooking and has a lovely 'bite'.

Once the pasta is laminated, begin to roll it out to your desired thickness. I like my ravioli nice and thin so I would go to the thinnest setting. For fettuccini and spaghetti I would go to the second or third thinnest setting. I go down gradually in thickness, two settings at a time to ensure my pasta sheets stay in tact.

Cook in salted boiling water for 2–3 minutes until al dente. It is best to use fresh pasta straight away, on the day you make it. Filled pastas can be frozen successfully.

Every year, Mum and I make this quince paste. This recipe is fail-safe and tastes incredible. We do finish it off differently—Mum dehydrates hers, while I just pop mine into sterilised jars after cooking it in the saucepan (quicker and just as good in my opinion). I will give you both endings—it's a choose your own cooking adventure.

- -

Quince Paste

makes 3–4 jars

1 kg (36 oz) quinces, washed
1 kg (36 oz) white (granulate) sugar
1 lemon, juiced

150 ml (5 fl oz) water
caster (superfine) sugar, for dusting (optional)

Preheat the oven to about 150°C (300°F).

Bake the quinces whole for approximately 2 hours until soft when pierced with a skewer. Remove and cool. When cool, peel and cut the quinces into quarters, removing the seeds.

Weigh the flesh and weigh out an equal amount of white sugar. Purée the flesh in a food processor (you may need to add a small amount of water to the purée as it could be quite thick) and then rub it through a sieve.

Put the weighed-out sugar, juice of 1 lemon and the water into a heavy-based saucepan. Bring to the boil and stir to dissolve the sugar. Add the quince pulp and cook over a very low heat for 2 hours, stirring occasionally with a wooden spoon. Towards the end, the paste will really thicken up and leave the sides of the saucepan when you are stirring.

Ending One
Pour the hot mixture into warm sterilised jars and screw the lid on tightly. Keep in a cool place. Once opened, keep in the refrigerator. This will keep for over a year in the refrigerator—I have a massive jar still going strong (I think I need to eat more cheese).

Ending Two
Spread the mixture thinly and evenly (no more than 5 mm/¼ in thick) in a shallow tray lined with baking paper and dry the paste in a 50°C (120°F) oven overnight. Cut the paste into small squares and dust with caster (superfine) sugar. Store between sheets of baking paper in an airtight container in the refrigerator. This also freezes very well.

This paste is fabulous with cheese and wine. It also makes an amazing glaze dredged over pork or turkey.

I have a lovely little kumquat tree that happily supplies me with a few jars of marmalade every year. I especially like the oval-shaped kumquats—I find their flavour a bit sweeter.

- -

Kumquat Marmalade

makes 6–8 jars

1 kg (36 oz) kumquats
1 litre (36 fl oz) water
1 kg (36 oz) white (granulated) sugar

Slice the kumquats very finely into thin pinwheels. Remove the seeds and put aside. Gather the seeds and put them in a muslin cloth and tie the top with string.

Put the kumquats, seed bag and water into a heavy-based saucepan and bring to the boil. Simmer for 30–60 minutes (depending how thinly you have sliced them), until the skin is soft. Remove the seed bag.

Add the sugar and simmer for another 30 minutes.

To see if the marmalade is ready, drop a small dollop onto a cold plate—if it tenses up and sets a bit, then it is ready. If it is not, simmer for another 10–20 minutes—this does vary so it's okay if it takes a few tests.

Once ready, pour the marmalade into sterilised jars. I hold the jar with a tea towel, to save my fingers from burning.

Lid and bam. Marmalade. This is great with Easy Awesome Bread and Homemade Butter (see Basics) and a nice cup of tea

Raspberries and strawberries are a huge favourite of mine and my nephew and nieces often perch behind my raised garden beds trying to eat them as fast as they can! The fruit grow wild and I try not to let them take over the garden, so they are also great to grow in pots. This recipe is so easy. I like to use blackberries or raspberries as there is very little preparation involved—no chopping, just smooshing. The flavour is nothing like the jam you would buy.

Berry Jam

makes about 3 cups

*2 cups raspberries or blackberries (make sure
    they are solid cups so smooth them down into
    the cup when you are measuring)*
2 cups sugar
2–3 tablespoons lemon juice

Combine all the ingredients in a heavy-based saucepan.

Bring to the boil and then simmer for 15–20 minutes until it thickens.

Pour into sterilised jars (but do you really think you are going to leave this on the shelf—I eat mine straight away).

The flavour is superb.

This chutney is phenomenal with cheddar cheese. Why not double and triple the quantity and give some away. This is too good to keep to yourself!

Spiced Pear and Pale Ale Chutney

makes about 600 ml/21 fl oz

2 onions, peeled and finely diced
1 clove garlic, finely chopped
sprig of thyme
2 tablespoons olive oil
½ teaspoon ground coriander
½ teaspoon ground cumin
½ teaspoon ground ginger
1 tablespoon mixed spice

1 whole star anise
½ cinnamon stick
4 pears, peeled, cored and diced
200 g (7 oz) sugar
330 ml (11 fl oz) pale ale
200 ml (7 fl oz) malt vinegar

Sauté onions, garlic and thyme in the olive oil until slightly soft. Add all of the spices and stir for a further minute. Add all of the remaining ingredients and simmer on a low heat, with a cartouche (see How to make a cartouche page 131) on the surface, until thick and golden, for a few minutes.

Pour into sterilised jars and seal.

This is an all-time favourite of mine, tried and trusted. It really is amazing on all sorts of savoury treats: poached eggs, toasted cheese, sausage rolls … anything that needs a little lift!

Tomato Kasundi

makes 4–6 jars

50 g (1¾ oz) fresh ginger, peeled
50 g (1¾ oz) cloves garlic, peeled
1 large onion, peeled and roughly chopped
2 long green chillies, halved and deseeded
½ cup vegetable oil
1 tablespoon black mustard seeds
2 sprigs curry leaves
1 tablespoon tumeric
2 tablespoons ground cumin
1 tablespoon smoked paprika
1 tablespoon dry mustard powder

½ cup brown malt vinegar
1½ kg (53 oz) tomatoes, washed and roughly chopped
1 cup sugar (any kind)
1½ tablespoons salt, to taste

In a food processor, blend the ginger, garlic, onion and chillies to a paste.

Pour half of the oil to a large pot and heat over a medium heat. Add all of the mustard seeds and fry until they pop. Add the curry leaves, stirring, as they will sputter a little. Add the remaining spices and the ginger and garlic paste and cook for another minute, until fragrant.

Add the remaining ingredients and bring to the boil. Reduce the heat to low and simmer for an hour, stirring occasionally, until thickened to the consistency of jam.

Spoon kasundi into sterilised jars and top with a little extra vegetable oil. Put on the lid and store in the refrigerator, or a cool spot. This improves with age—I try to leave it for at least a month, if I can.

A Homegrown Table

This has quite a bit of heat, so if you like it with a bit less heat, add less chilli powder. This is delicious on savory pastry treats and on egg-based dishes.

- -

Spicy Eggplant (Aubergine) Kasundi

1 bulb garlic
8 tablespoons chilli powder
3 tablespoons ground cumin
1½ tablespoons ground mustard
2 tablespoons ground fenugreek
2 tablespoons turmeric
1 cup malt vinegar
1½ cups grapeseed oil
1 kg (36 oz) eggplant (aubergine)
10 tablespoons white (granulated) sugar
3 tablespoons salt

Peel and roughly pound the garlic in a mortar and pestle. Mix all the powders with the vinegar.

Heat the oil in a frying pan over a medium heat. Add the crushed garlic. When slightly coloured, add the powder mixture and mix well.

Cut the eggplant into 1 cm (½ in) cubes and add to the spice mixture. Add the sugar and the salt. Stir until the sugar is dissolved. Cook down for about 45 minutes.

Pour into sterilised jars and put the lid on. Store in the refrigerator or a cool spot. This only improves with age. It is quite spicy so if you like less spice, go easy on the chilli powder.

These are so cheap and easy to make, and will transform the dishes that you use them in!

- -

Preserved Lemons

*12 thin-skinned juicy lemons (I like Meyer,
    but any sort will be okay)*
1 cup sea salt
2–3 cinnamon sticks, broken into shards
1 tablespoon coriander seeds
extra lemon juice, may be needed

Wash the lemons well in hot water.

Cut the stalk end off each lemon, and cut the lemons into quarters. Put them in a large bowl. Lightly squeeze each quarter to release some of the juices. Mix in the salt roughly to encourage more juice to be released (I find wearing rubber gloves useful to prevent stinging).

Pack the lemon quarters into sterilised jars and squash down as much as possible. Pour in the salty juice as well. Leave overnight in the refrigerator. The next day, push the lemons down more (this will be easier as the lemons will start to soften). Add a few shards of cinnamon stick and a few coriander seeds.

If the lemons are not submerged in their own juices, then add some juice from extra squeezed lemons—I usually find this is not necessary.

Make sure the jar is full of juice and there is no air left. Cap with a plastic lid. Metal ones will corrode. Keep in the refrigerator or a cool place for 4–6 weeks before using and will last for up to a year.

To use, remove the pith, then rinse and slice the peel. Use it under my Roast Chicken Stuffed Three Ways (see recipe page 161) or add a few slices into the Olive Tapenade (see recipe page 170).

This is incredible! I love how you can turn a simple salmon fillet into something very special just by smoking it. The flavour of this smoked salmon is out of this world. Works for trout too.

- -

Double Tea-smoked Salmon

serves 4

600 g (21 oz) salt
400 g (14 oz) sugar
zest of 1 lemon
1 x 400 g (14 oz) large fillet of salmon or trout, from the body not the tail

wood chips (or smoking shavings)
tea (I like lapsang souchang, as it is already quite smoky)

Mix together the salt and sugar. Add the lemon zest.

Cure the fish by rubbing in the salt mixture so that all surfaces are covered. Place the fish in a long dish and pour over all of the curing mixture. Cover with cling film and refrigerate overnight and into the next day—for about 16–20 hours.

Remove the fish, rinse it off and pat dry. Put the fish back into the refrigerator, uncovered, to dry it out a little bit, for about 3 hours.

Prepare the smoking kit. I use my stainless steel saucepan with steamer insert with lid. You will also need a small saucer that fits loosely into the steamer insert, to allow the smoke to get through with a lid.

Dry fry a handful of wood shavings and half a handful of lapsang souchong tea in a separate heavy cast-iron frying pan (don't use a non-stick pan for this, you may ruin it). Put the frying pan on as high a heat as you can. Do not leave this pan alone!

While doing that, put a saucer into the steamer insert and put ice cubes on top of the saucer. Place the salmon on top of the ice cubes and put the lid on the steamer insert to seal it. Cling film the lid onto the steamer insert to seal it.

A Homegrown Table

236

Double Tea-smoked Salmon (cont.)

- -

After 3–4 minutes the smoke from the chips will be intense (I even wait for mine to catch on fire but only do this if you feel confident). Transfer the smoking chips and tea into the foil-lined saucepan and place the prepared steamer on top and cling film the lid of the steamer insert to the saucepan to create an airtight smoker.

Leave for 20–30 minutes. If you want to double-smoke the salmon, repeat the entire smoking process.

- -

Pickling Solution

100 g (3½ oz) white sugar
100 ml (3½ oz) white wine vinegar
100 ml (3½ oz) water

Combine all ingredients in a pan and heat until the sugar dissolves. Remove from the heat and use the liquid to pickle different vegetables.

Pickled Red Onion

100 g (3½ oz) white (granulated) sugar
100 ml (3½ oz) red wine vinegar
100 ml (3½ oz) water
1 red onion, quartered and petals separated

Combine the sugar, vinegar and water into a pan and heat until the sugar dissolves.

Place onion petals into the hot pickling solution and then leave it to cool.

Pickled Cucumber

2 short Lebanese cucumbers
100 ml (3½ fl oz) water
100 ml (3½ fl oz) white wine vinegar
100 g (3½ oz) white (granulated) sugar

To pickle cucumber, mix the water, white wine and sugar together in a saucepan. Bring the mixture to the boil and dissolve the sugar. Turn off and leave to cool to room temperature.

Using a potato peeler, peel long lengths of cucumber into ribbons. Don't include the seeds—once you start peeling near the core stop. Place the ribbons into the pickling water for 5–10 minutes then drain.

Pickled Mushrooms

Add sliced mushrooms to hot pickling solution and allow to cool. Once cool, the pickled mushrooms will be ready to use.

Dry-cured Bacon

1.3 kg (2.9 lb) piece free-range pork belly,
   skin on, de-boned

CURE
350 g (12 oz) coarse sea salt
185 g (6 oz) soft brown sugar
2 teaspoons coarsely cracked black pepper
sprig of rosemary, chopped
2 bay leaves, crushed
2 fennel seeds, crushed

Find a suitable plastic vessel to hold the pork in the fridge. Don't use metal, as it will rust.

Mix all the cure ingredients together.

Take a handful of cure and rub it into all surfaces of the pork belly. Place the pork in the plastic container in the refrigerator and every day for 6 days rub in another handful of cure into all sides. Drain off the excess liquid each day as necessary.

At the end of six days you will have beautiful home-cured free-range bacon. Brush off excess salt, slice as required and enjoy.

My sister Katherine makes this and does it ever pack a punch! But if, like me, you love garlic, then go with this dressing. It is great just on leafy greens. You can also add some cucumber and fennel for a delicious cool summer salad to go with roasted meats and a barbecue—yumbo!

Delicious Garlicky Vinaigrette

1–2 cloves garlic
2 teaspoons flaked salt

juice of 1 lemon
¼ cup olive oil

Grind the garlic and salt together in a mortar and pestle. Add the lemon juice and grind. Mix in the olive oil.

This is enough for one large green salad. Store excess in the refrigerator for up to 1 week.

Basic Vinaigrette

1 teaspoon Dijon mustard
2 tablespoons best vinegar (cider or white wine)
pinch of salt

150 ml (5 fl oz) good-quality extra virgin olive oil
1 tablespoon lemon juice

Whisk together all the ingredients in a bowl and pour into a jar or bottle with a lid. Keep in the fridge, for up to one week, and shake before each use.

Easy Lemon Dressing

1 part lemon juice
4 parts extra virgin olive oil

pinch of salt

Whisk together all the ingredients in a bowl and pour into a jar or bottle with a lid. Keep in the fridge, for up to one week, and shake before each use.

Raspberry Vinegar

2 cups raspberries
1 litre (36 fl oz) white wine vinegar

Put the raspberries into a large jar big enough to hold everything. Pour vinegar over the top of the raspberries and seal with a lid. Leave for 2 weeks.

After 2 weeks, the raspberries will look pale and the vinegar will have taken on most of the colour.

Strain through a muslin cloth and decant into pretty bottles.

makes 2 500 ml (1 pint) jars

Basics

This is my regular mayonnaise recipe. It is so easy to make. It is probably technically a dijonaise but I use it as mayonnaise.

Homemade Mayonnaise

2 egg yolks
1 clove garlic
juice of 1 lemon
1 tablespoon Dijon mustard
2 good pinches of salt
dash of water
50 ml (1¾ fl oz) extra virgin olive oil,
   combined with 300 ml (10½ fl oz)
   grapeseed oil

In a small food processor, blend the yolks, garlic, lemon juice, Dijon mustard, salt, and a dash of water until well mixed and a little bit foamy.

Blend in the oil, 50 ml (1¾ fl oz) at a time, blending well between each addition to make sure it emulsifies. I find it easy just to put the oil in a measuring jug and pour in approximately 50 ml (1¾ fl oz) at a time—you don't have to be exact.

Variations
Use a few cloves of roast garlic instead of fresh garlic.

Chop in fresh dill if you want to spread over fish.

Chop in fresh tarragon to serve the mayonnaise with cold chicken.

Blend in a chipotle chilli.

This tomato sauce is truly the taste of good old-fashioned hospitality! You obviously need lots of bottles for this! And a big pot, although you can cook it in batches.

Tomato Sauce

7.2 kg (15 lb 4 oz) tomatoes
1.5 kg (3 lb 5 oz) white (granulated) sugar
700 ml (24 fl oz) brown vinegar
28 g whole cloves
1 teaspoon cayenne pepper
85 g (3 oz) garlic, chopped
4 tablespoons salt
1 tablespoon ground ginger

Cut up the tomatoes and garlic, sprinkle with salt and leave overnight. Drain off most of the juice.

Add all other ingredients, and boil for 3 hours.

Strain and bottle in sterilised bottles. Keeps for several months in a cool dark place.

Making your own stock, which you can turn into lovely jus, is worth the effort. Homemade stock is what makes food taste so good in restaurants!

- -

My Rich and Luxurious Jus (aka Veal Stock)

2 kg (70 fl oz) beef marrow bones and
rib bones
4 tomatoes
vegetable oil, for frying
1 brown onion, peeled and chopped
1 stick celery, chopped
½ leek, chopped
1 carrot, chopped
100 g (3½ oz) bacon trimmings
100 g (3½ oz) beef trimmings

½ bottle red wine
shot of cognac
½ split pig's trotter
½ bulb garlic
pinch peppercorns
pinch of fresh thyme
2 bay leaves
water, to cover (about 4 litres/8¾ pints)
lemon juice, to taste
salt and pepper, to taste

Preheat the oven to 180°C (350°F) and roast the beef bones for 30–40 minutes until golden. Cut the tomatoes in half and pan-roast them face down until blackened in a separate pan.

In a large saucepan, heat some vegetable oil and caramelise the onion, celery, leek, carrot, one by one in the same pan. Remove from the pan and set aside.

In a large saucepan, fry the bacon and beef trim in a little vegetable oil. Deglaze with the red wine and cognac and boil to reduce to a syrup.

Add all the cooked ingredients, including the beef bones, and the rest of the ingredients, to the red wine reduction. Bring gently to a simmer and cook at just below the boil for 6–8 hours (or 3 hours in a pressure cooker).

Pass through a fine sieve, reserving the liquid and discarding all the solids.

Pour the liquid into a pan and reduce it to desired consistency, either as a light stock for braising or reduced to a gelatinous-velvety-shiny-dark sauce. Adjust and finish the jus using lemon, salt and pepper to taste. This can be frozen.

Simple Stock

2 kg (70 oz) beef marrow bones
olive oil, for frying
1 brown onion, peeled and chopped
1 stick celery, chopped
1 carrot, chopped
½ bulb garlic, roughly chopped with skin on

2 tomatoes, chopped
½ bottle red wine
pinch peppercorns
pinch of thyme
2 bay leaves
water, to cover (about 4 litres/8¾ pints)

Roast the marrow bones in a 180°C (350°F) oven for 30–40 minutes. Meanwhile, heat the oil in a pan and sauté the onion, carrot, celery and garlic, until soft.

Transfer marrow bones, sautéed vegetables and the remaining ingredients into a pressure cooker and cook at pressure for 3 hours. If you don't have a pressure cooker, transfer the ingredients to a large stock pot and bring to a simmer. Cook at just below the boil for 6–8 hours.

Leave to cool slightly, and strain. This can be frozen.

Vegetable Stock

1 tablespoon olive oil
1 onion, roughly chopped
3 cloves garlic, roughly chopped
1 carrot, roughly chopped

1 leek, roughly chopped
2 celery sticks, roughly chopped
1.5 litres (52 fl oz) water

Heat 1 tablespoon of the olive oil in a large saucepan set over medium heat.

Add onion and garlic and cook for 5 minutes or until golden, stirring regularly. Add the carrot, leek, celery, cover with the water and bring to the boil. Reduce heat to a simmer and cook for 30 minutes with the lid on.

Strain the stock through a fine sieve. Can be frozen.

Brown Chicken Stock

1 free-range chicken carcass, cut into 8 pieces
4 cloves garlic
1 eschalot (shallot)
olive oil, for frying
1 small carrot, chopped
2 celery stalks, chopped
2 sprigs thyme
6 peppercorns

Preheat the oven to 180°C (350°F).

Roast the chicken pieces for 30 minutes until brown.

In a large saucepan, sauté the garlic cloves and eschalot in olive oil for a few minutes, until brown. Add in the chicken pieces, carrot, celery, thyme and pepper.

Cover with water and bring to the boil. Simmer for 90 minutes. Or do this step in the pressure cooker for about 30 minutes at pressure.

Strain the solids and keep the liquid. This is good to freeze, or use immediately in various recipes in this book.

Ham Hock Stock

1 tablespoon extra virgin olive oil
3 cloves garlic, chopped
1 eschalot (shallot), peeled and chopped
1 bunch thyme
1 ham hock
2 litres (70 fl oz) water

Heat the olive oil in a large pan. Sauté the garlic and eschalot on medium heat for a few minutes, then add the thyme and ham hock.

Cover the ham hock with water and bring to the boil. Reduce to a simmer and simmer until the meat falls off the bone—about 2 hours. Skim impurities off the surface every so often.

Cool and scrape off the fat that has solidified on the top. Use the stock for the delicious Nettle and Broadbean Soup on page 68, or where ever takes your fancy where you want more of a bacon flavour. You can freeze this for up to 3 months.

Acknowledgements

I would really like to thank George Calombaris, Gary Mehigan and Matt Preston—without your tough love and ongoing support I could not have made it this far. I would also like to thank the entire MasterChef team for their help and support and tireless work in putting it all together.

I want to thank my family: Ian, Rosie, Rachel, Katherine, Jet, Richard, and my inspiring nephew and nieces Max, Ada and Zoe, and wonderful Dan. I would also like to thank my wonderful and talented girlfriends: Lil Smith (you have been incredible in this whole process Lil—thank you so much), Joanne Garden, Anna Benbow, Meg Butler, Amber Davies, Jacoba Kelly, Michelle Bolitho, Shaye Bradbury, Juliette Begg and Sue Neale for keeping me sane. I love you Gemma Jones and Pip Lincolne—thanks.

Also, Peter Traianou, Uncle Stack, Aleks Svazas, Anne Prime, Kay Giovanetti, Ross Benbow, and David Bloom. Thank you Lynton Tapp for being with me in this journey right to the end of the show and beyond. Thank you to my new food-found friends who I know will be around for a while—Annie Smithers, Matt Germanchis, Kylie Millar, Mark Hannel, Gary's Meats at Prahran Market, Anthony and Lisa Key from Key Ingredients, Alice Zaslavsky, Julia Taylor, Adam Liaw, Kate Bracks, Andy Allen, Julie Goodwin, Mark Hannel, The Fruit Peddlers in Northcote (www.terramadre.com.au), The Truffle Man–The Marshall Family, Braidwood, Kitten Smithers, Kate Olssen, Sue Stubbs and Lliane Clarke for your tireless and inspiring work. Thanks to Louise Spargo and Dennerly Healy for looking after us in the MasterChef House, and finally, the MasterChef Class of 2013, I have learnt so much from everybody, and I thank you for all of your love, support and cuddles!

Index

First published in 2013 by
New Holland Publishers
London • Sydney • Cape Town • Auckland
www.newhollandpublishers.com

The Chandlery Unit 114 50 Westminster Bridge Road London SE1 7QY
1/66 Gibbes Street Chatswood NSW 2067 Australia
Wembley Square First Floor Solan Road Gardens Cape Town 8001 South Africa
218 Lake Road Northcote Auckland New Zealand

A catalogue record of this book is available at the British Library and at the National Library of Australia

ISBN: 9781742574714

10 9 8 7 6 5 4 3 2 1

Managing Director : Fiona Schultz
Publisher: Diane Ward
Project editor: Jodi De Vantier
Designer: Tracy Loughlin
Stylist: Kate Olsson
Photographer: Sue Stubbs
Production Director: Olga Dementiev
Printer: Toppan Leefung Printing Limited

Follow New Holland Publishers on
Facebook: www.facebook.com/NewHollandPublishers